A Special Sisterhood:

100 Fascinating Women From History Who Never Had Children

Laura Carroll

Illustrations by Nataliia Tonyeva

ISBN 978-0-9863832-4-3 (epub)

ISBN 978-0-9863832-7-4 (paperback)

Jacket design by Lisa DeSpain

To my special sisters
past and present
whose unique lives
have not included motherhood.

Contents

Welcome to the Tip of the Iceberg

What is one of the biggest things girls learn they'll do when they grow up? Have children. That is what women are destined to do—become mothers, right? Wrong. Not now or in history. Going back many generations, there have been many reasons why women's lives have not included motherhood. Some chose it, some didn't. Of the countless ways women end up not having children, some are just busy living awesome lives!

Then and now, all women who have not had children have this major thing in common and form a special sisterhood. And there are lots of us. I mean lots. This book is just the tip of the iceberg of the thousands of examples of women from history who had amazing lives without having had children. Choosing just 100 for this book was a difficult task!

As you'll see, the following snapshots of 100 women's lives do not talk about why they did not have children (for the most part). Instead, this book focuses on the lives they lived. It also does not only feature very famous women you may have already heard about. For example, the well-known deaf author and activist Helen Keller never had children. Neither did Rosa Parks, who would not move from her seat on the bus which helped ignite the Civil Rights movement. This is also true for authors Louisa May Alcott (*Little*

Women) and Emily Dickinson (famous poet) as well. And there are so many more.

Instead, *A Special Sisterhood* introduces you to fascinating women from history without children you may be less likely to have heard of or know much about. It starts with Goddesses based in mythology who are not real in the human sense and were worshipped long ago. From then on, all women in *A Special Sisterhood* were real. I hope these snapshots of their life stories make you want to know more about them. You will easily find more information about all of them online.

It is so common to think that all women are destined to become mothers and that motherhood is the ultimate way for women to have a fulfilling life. These women are but 100 examples that tell the true story. For those who want to become mothers, that is great. They join those, now and in the past, who did too. For those whose lives unfold such that they don't have children, for whatever reasons, they too join a special sisterhood starting very far back to today. It's time for people to know more about them, and *A Special Sisterhood* sets out to do just that.

Like it did for me, may the women in this book inspire you to continue to learn about more women, alive now and from history, for whom motherhood did not play a part in their remarkable lives. And may their lives show you that ultimately, your life is uniquely yours to create!

Goddesses

Goddess of Hearth and Home

Hestia

In ancient Greek religion and mythology, Hestia is the goddess of the hearth, which is a fireplace in one's home, and can mean one's home in general. She is one of the Twelve Olympians, which is the set of major gods to have lived on Mount Olympus. From the private to public, she watched over home lives and family. In Greek times in people's homes, Hestia was honored as part of important rituals, such as births and deaths of family members. Her devotion to hearth and home also included being a warm and generous neighbor and helping those in need. If one did not give food and/or shelter when it was needed, it was considered a crime against Hestia. At public events and important civic functions, sacrifices in her honor were made at cities' communal hearths, with Hestia's flames, which were not allowed to ever burn out. She had a presence in every town, and people moving to new areas would take a flame in her honor from their old town to their new one. Although gods fell in love with her and wanted her hand in marriage, she swore a great oath that she would remain a virgin and never marry. Then and now, Hestia was and can be honored through simple acts, such as lighting a candle dedicated to her. If you don't have a fireplace, you can light it in the part of your home that feels like the heart of your home. One can also bring this special goddess' caring and protective spirit to any kind of home-related project.

The Virgin Huntress

Artemis

Artemis was the daughter of Zeus, the king of all gods in ancient Greek religion and mythology. As the legend goes, when she was three years old her father asked her what gifts she would like from him. Artemis had many things she wanted and was very specific. Knowing her father's power, the gifts she asked for included eternal virginity. It is written that Artemis was against marriage, believing it stripped women of their power. She also wished for a bow and arrow like his, a knee-length saffron tunic with a red hem to wear when she was hunting, sixty ocean nymphs, twenty river nymphs to take care of her boots and feed her hounds when she was hunting, all the mountains in the world, and only one city, as she intended to live most of her life in the mountains. In addition to being known as the virgin huntress, Artemis is the goddess of animals, wilderness, childbirth, and protectress of girls up to the age of marriage. In addition to being a fierce protector, she was also known to be quite brutal if anyone attempted to dishonor her in any way. In 262 BC a temple named after her was destroyed by the Goths, a group that played a major role in the fall of the Roman Empire. Only one column is still standing on the site. A temple named The Temple of Artemis was since erected in her honor in what is now western Turkey.

Goddess of a Thousand Works

Minerva

Minerva was the Roman goddess of wisdom, art, poetry, philosophy, crafts, medicine, and commerce. She ruled over so many different aspects of life that she has been referred to as the 'goddess of a thousand works.' Minerva was the wisest of all the Roman gods and goddesses and had a very strategic mind. Even the Romans associated her name with the Latin word 'mens' which means 'mind.' Minerva was dedicated to remaining a virgin, refused the advances of gods, and never married. There were many temples dedicated to her in the Roman Empire, but the top one was on Aventine Hill, one of the seven hills on which ancient Rome was built. It was a meeting place for actors, writers, and craftspeople. There were also many festivals dedicated to Minerva. The biggest one was called Quinquatria, lasted five days, and included poet and theater performances and battles with gladiators, professional fighters of the day. One of the most impressive statues of her is ten feet tall in the Capitoline Museums in Rome. She is also honored on the state seal of the state of California, which shows this powerful goddess seated with the California Grizzly Bear at her feet.

High Powered Leaders

Leading Britain to Become a World Power

Queen Elizabeth I
(1533-1603)

Queen Elizabeth I was born into English royalty. Her father was King Henry VIII and her mother was his second wife. After her father's death, two of her half-siblings reigned before Elizabeth took the throne at the age of twenty-five. She had her father's charisma, was a popular queen, and inspired loyalty. She was strong-willed, very intelligent, and she spoke multiple languages, including Welsh, Greek, Latin, Spanish, French, and Italian. During her forty-four-year reign, literature and music boomed in England. As Queen, she dealt with war and trade issues with the Netherlands, France, Spain, Ireland, Russia, Muslim states, and America. A famous battle between Spain and England in 1588 became one of her biggest victories. An undefeated 130-ship naval fleet called the Spanish Armada tried to invade England, and England won. Queen Elizabeth I's strengths also included her decision not to marry and be celibate. In her day, this was very strange, but in her case, it was a courageous and revolutionary choice. Those who have studied her life say that the biggest reason she did not want to marry and to stay celibate was because she feared she would lose her independence. The Queen knew that marriage and motherhood would erode her power. It has also been written that she may very well have feared childbirth. Two of Queen Elizabeth I's stepmothers, her grandmother, and several acquaintances died in childbirth. When it came to marriage, she described herself as married to her kingdom. Queen Elizabeth's reign is known as The Golden Age, a time when Britain emerged as a world power.

Dedicated Leader of the
People of Hawaii

Queen Lili'uokalani
(1838-1917)

Queen Lili'uokalani's birth name was Lydia Kamaka'eha. Born into Hawaiian royalty, she was very studious and intelligent. She was also an excellent musician and composer and knew traditional Hawaiian chant and prose. In her lifetime, Lili'uokalani composed more than 150 songs, including the popular, "Aloha 'Oe." Her older brother became king of Hawaii in 1874 and named her younger brother the heir to the throne. But he died, and at the age of thirty-nine, she became the crown princess, known with the royal name, Lili'uokalani. When she took the throne, a new Hawaiian constitution had been forced on the Hawaiian people by wealthy sugar planters and businessmen. Queen Lili'uokalani fought to change this and give the power back to the Hawaiian people. Unfortunately, the sugar planters and businessmen forced the Queen to surrender the Hawaiian Kingdom to the United States in 1893. She went to prison for eight months and appealed to the president at the time, President Grover Cleveland, to restore her to power. He supported this and tried to negotiate putting the Queen and the monarchy back in power. The next president, William McKinley, did not support this, and when he was elected, the United States officially took over Hawaii. She tells her story in her autobiography, *Hawaii's Story by Hawaii's Queen.* Queen Lili'uokalani's commitment to the Hawaiian people remained for the rest of her life. In her will, she left her estate to help orphaned Native Hawaiian children and other children in need. When she was seventy-one years old, the Lili'uokalani Trust was formed for this legacy of generosity to live on. Loved and respected by her people, Queen Lili'uokalani was a model of loyalty to the people of Hawaii.

Influential Ethiopian Empress

Taytu Betul
(1851-1918)

Taytu Betul's noble family dated back to the 1600s of the Ethiopian dynasty. Taytu was educated, which was highly unusual for an Ethiopian woman at the time. She could read and write Amharic, the official language of Ethiopia, which is descended from the ancient language, Ge'ez, which she also fluently spoke. In her late thirties, her husband, King Menelik of Shewa, rose to the throne and she became Empress of Ethiopia. She was a valuable advisor to her husband, and she helped him make important decisions for their country. One such decision related to what is known as the "Scramble for Africa." Beginning in the 1880s, European countries took control of most African countries. Italy wanted to take Ethiopia, and Empress Taytu convinced her husband to fight. Empress Taytu was a force behind mobilizing thousands of men and women to take part in the fighting and care for their wounded soldiers. And she was on the frontline of the battlefield herself. In the fight against Italian troops, she commanded over 5,000 Ethiopian troops. Ethiopia won, making this one of the most significant victories of African armies battling European countries at the time. Taytu also founded Addis Ababa, Ethiopia's capital city, which is still the capital today. When the King started to have health issues, Empress Taytu began to make decisions on his behalf. Many people did not like this, and Empress Taytu was ultimately forced out of this role and into retirement. She is remembered as a brave and strong-willed Empress dedicated to her country at a critical time in its history.

Power Player in Shaping the Middle East

Gertrude Bell
(1868-1926)

Gertrude Bell started life in County Durham, England. She was from a wealthy family and got her degree from Oxford University. Gertrude was very adventurous. As a young woman, she traveled to many places, and at the age of twenty-four, went to Iran for the first time. She fell in love with it and the Middle East. She went to many countries in the Middle East and wrote books about it. Because of Gertrude's expert knowledge of the area, during World War I the British government hired her to gather information about certain tribes in the Middle East. In her late forties, she was made Commander of the Order of the British Empire, a high-level title given to those who have important national roles. After the war, Gertrude attended the 1921 Conference with British Middle East experts and England's then secretary of state, Winston Churchill, and was involved in establishing the country boundaries of Iraq. Gertrude also helped Faysal I become the new king of Iraq. She was a trusted advisor to him and played the role of mediator between his and British governments. Because of her importance to King Faysal, she gained the nickname, "The Uncrowned Queen of Iraq." In the building of Iraq, she was committed to involving the local tribes and creating schools and hospitals for women. In addition to international relations, Gertrude was amazing in other ways. She was an accomplished archeologist and mountain climber, traveled around the world twice, and was the first European woman to travel alone for hundreds of miles in the Arabian desert.

Pioneer for Women Workers' Rights

Margaret Bondfield
(1873-1953)

Margaret Bondfield was born in Somerset, England, into a family of humble means. Her father was a lacemaker and was active in political organizations wanting to protect the rights of working men. When Margaret was fourteen years old, she left home to become an assistant at a fabric shop. Little did she know that this would shape the rest of her life. At twenty-one Margaret moved to another town to do the same, and the working conditions and poor pay there led her to London, where she hoped to find a better working environment. But conditions were even worse. This inspired her to become a trade union member and activist. In her thirties, Gertrude helped found the National Federation of Women Workers. Wanting to improve the working conditions and salaries of working women also led her to be involved in women's fight for equality and the right to vote. She became the first woman chairman of the Trades Union Congress, a national organization of British trade unions. At forty-nine years old, she made history when she was appointed Parliamentary Secretary to the Minister for Labour. Five years later, she became the first woman to be a British Cabinet Minister, the Minister of Labour. She received an honorary Doctor of Laws degree and a noteworthy citizen honor called the "Freedom of the Borough" from her hometown of Chard. Margaret was a pioneer in women's labor rights and broke barriers in male-dominated unions and political positions in England.

The First Woman Elected
to the United States Congress

Jeannette Rankin
(1880-1973)

Jeannette Rankin was from Montana, United States. Her parents ran a large, successful ranch. Growing up Jeannette worked on the ranch and saw how men and women worked as equals there but how women weren't treated equally when it came to the right to vote. At twenty-two years old, she got her degree in biology and worked as a teacher and social worker before getting involved in the movement to give women the right to vote in the state of Washington. It was made an amendment to the Washington state constitution in 1910. Jeannette then went on to help the same thing happen in Montana in 1914. Next, in her thirties, she ran for a seat in the United States House of Representatives and won, becoming the first woman in the United States Congress. Think about this achievement—Jeannette was elected to Congress before the United States Constitution's 19th Amendment, the Women's Right to Vote, was made official! In her late fifties, she ran again and won. During these separate terms, she helped pass the 19th Amendment. During her terms in office, Jeannette also worked to help the welfare of mothers and children. On matters of war, Jeannette made brave votes that did not line up with her congressional colleagues. She did not believe in war and voted against both World War I and World War II. The World War II vote was 388 for to 1 against, and she was the '1.' After leaving office, Jeannette continued to speak out against war. During the 1960s, she led the "Jeannette Rankin Peace Brigade," a 5,000-person protest march in Washington, D.C., against the Vietnam War. A groundbreaking Congressperson, Jeannette is also remembered for her achievements in social welfare and women's rights and her unswerving stance for peace.

Dedicated to Her Māori People

Te Puea Hērangi
(1883-1952)

Of royal Māori descent, Te Puea Hērangi was born in the Waikato District on the upper North Island of New Zealand. The Māori people were indigenous Polynesians who settled in New Zealand. Her grandfather was the second Māori King, and her uncle the third. Early in her life, her uncle saw that she had special abilities and educated her about her Māori people and traditions. She went to college and was fluent in her native language as well as English. In her late twenties, as a royal, Te Puea began to do many great things for her Tainui people, the Māori from the central western part of the north island of New Zealand. She fought against and protected Māori who refused to join the New Zealand Army during World War I. Te Puea became a leader in the Kingitanga Movement, which brought tribal communities together to protect their communities, culture, and resources. In 1918, there was a terrible smallpox epidemic, and Te Puea established a settlement called Turangawaewae, where many people and orphans could heal. She became nationally known, and in newspapers, she was often called Princess Te Puea, which she did not like because the role of princess does not exist in the Māori culture. Nonetheless, for many years as a leader for her people, Te Puea worked hard to strengthen her people's economic lives. They say that her spirit can still be felt in the meeting house at Turangawaewae.

The First Black Woman Elected to the United States Congress

Shirley Chisholm
(1924-2005)

Shirley Chisholm's life began in New York, United States, to parents who had immigrated from Barbados. When she was very young, she and her sisters lived with their grandmother in Barbados while her parents worked in New York. When she was ten years old, she returned to New York during the Great Depression, so life was hard for her family. After graduating from high school, Shirley went to Brooklyn College, was a star student, an excellent debater, and majored in sociology. At age twenty-eight, she got her master's degree in elementary education at Columbia University. While working in this field, Shirley got involved in local politics and decided this was her future. At age forty, she was elected to the New York State Assembly, one of the houses in the New York State Legislature. Four years later, she was elected to the U.S. House of Representatives, making her the first black woman elected to the U.S. Congress. She would go on to be re-elected for six more terms. At the age of forty-eight, she did something that had not been done before—she ran in the U.S. Presidential primaries. During her campaign, she survived three assassination attempts. As a black woman, she did not expect to be nominated for the Democratic candidate for president but wanted her campaign to spark change for the future. Over her political career, Shirley fought for education opportunities, healthcare, equal rights, and social justice. She wrote two autobiographies and wanted to be remembered as having guts and being a catalyst for change in America. She received many recognitions, including the Presidential Medal of Freedom, the highest United States civilian award. Shirley Chisholm State Park, with its great views of New York City, also honors Shirley and her bold, trailblazing life.

Passionate Patriot of Madagascar

Gisèle Rabesahala
(1929-2011)

Gisèle Rabesahala was born in Madagascar, Africa. When she was a girl, France ruled Madagascar and her father was in the French army. During his service she and her family lived in France, Tunisia, and what is now Mali, Africa. When Gisèle was thirteen, her father died, and she went back to Madagascar. She was lucky to get a high school education because not many Malagasy women were able to at the time. At the age of seventeen, Gisèle became a secretary for an organization called the Democratic Movement for Malagasy Renewal. It wanted Madagascar to become its own nation again and no longer be ruled by France. In her early twenties, she created the Madagascar Solidarity Committee to support victims of the repression, political prisoners, and their families. She also co-founded the *Imongo Vaovao* newspaper, which promoted Madagascar's struggle for independence. Gisèle became known as a young woman of excellent political abilities in a world dominated by men. She was the first woman elected to local Madagascan government, and not that long after, became her political party's leader. In 1960, Madagascar gained independence, but not completely. Gisèle continued to fight for true independence and against social inequalities in her country. When she was forty-eight, she became the first woman-appointed minister in Madagascar. As Minister of Culture and Revolutionary Art, for fourteen years she worked on many efforts to preserve her country's culture and educate the people. Gisèle dedicated her life to the independence and human rights of the Madagascan people and was a major force in her country's political history.

Moxie & Muscle

Adventurous Swordfighter & More

Julie d'Aubigny
(circa 1670-1707)

An only child raised by her father, Julie d'Aubigny was born and grew up in Versailles, France. Her father worked for King Louis XIV and had her educated by the tutors of the king's servants. In her early teens, she also learned to swordfight. Her father was an accomplished swordsman who trained the king's servants and insisted she learn to fence from the masters at the time. Julie excelled at it and dueled only with men. In her teens, she fell in love with her fencing master, who had killed a man in an illegal duel. He had to flee, and adventurous Julie put on men's clothes and left with him. To make money, they gave fencing exhibitions in taverns, advertising her as a woman though dressed as a man. One time when an onlooker called out that she really was a man, Julie tore open her shirt to settle the matter! She and her lover had great voices so they added singing to their shows. While the relationship did not last, her passion for fencing would remain. Despite anti-dueling laws in France, Julie won duels with many men and got pardons on the clever grounds that the laws only mentioned men. Singing would also be a passion. Her singing success on the road inspired her to want to be in the Paris opera. Julie landed an audition for the Marseille Academy of Music and passed. So in addition to being the most famous female swordfighter, from her late twenties to mid-thirties she also made her fame as a singer. In these two adventurous tracks in life, and many escapades in between, Julie carved her own path despite the social norms of 17th century France.

First Woman to Swim
the English Channel

Gertrude Ederle
(1905-2003)

From New York, United States, Gertrude Ederle was a tomboy as a child. Her father, who owned a butcher shop, taught her to swim at their family's summer cottage. When she was thirteen years old, Gertrude joined the Women's Swimming Association in New York City. It was not long before it was clear she would go places in swimming when she won national championships in the 220-yard and 440-yard swim. At age sixteen, she won a big race across the New York Bay called the J.P. Day Cup. She started setting amateur world records in 100-500 meter races. By age eighteen, Gertrude made the American Olympic team and won two bronze medals and a gold. Her next big challenge: the English Channel (the Atlantic Ocean on the south coast of the United Kingdom and the northeast of France). On her first try, she swam the breaststroke and did not finish. But on her second, with a former English Channel swimmer as a coach, she not only finished using the crawl stroke, but set a world record as the first woman to complete the English Channel and the fastest recorded time to date. She became known as the "Queen of the Waves," and blasted myths that women were the "weaker sex." When Gertrude came home, more than two million people lined the streets for the parade in her honor. She was inducted into the International Swimming Hall of Fame and the National Women's Hall of Fame. By her thirties, she had lost most of her hearing and spent her later years teaching deaf children how to swim. Gertrude showed what grit, determination, and endurance can do. In her case, it meant making swimming history!

The Highest-Ranking Woman in Judo

Keiko Fukuda
(1913-2013)

The granddaughter of a jujitsu master, Keiko Fukuda started her life in Tokyo, Japan. As a girl, she was raised in traditional Japanese culture for women. She knew about the martial art of jujitsu because of her grandfather, and one day when she watched a training session, Keiko became so fascinated she decided to learn it herself, which was very rare for females to do then. Her father had died, and her mother supported her, thinking she would eventually quit when marrying a judo practitioner. Keiko would end up doing nothing of the kind. After getting a college degree in Japanese literature, at age twenty-one, a man named Kanō Jigorō invited her to the judo school he founded called Kodokan. While very unusual, he had been one of her grandfather's jujitsu students. He asked Keiko to come to the school as an act of respect for her grandfather. In a very small group of women in the school then, by age twenty-four Keiko became a judo instructor. She would teach and be loved by her students for the rest of her ninety-nine-year life. At just under five feet tall, Keiko would achieve the highest degree black belt, but not without controversy. By her late thirties, she had her fifth degree black belt. For twenty years, the Kodokan refused to give her the sixth degree black belt. By her nineties, she had her ninth degree black belt, the highest rank the Kodokan ever gave to a woman. When Keiko was ninety-eight, USA Judo gave her the tenth, the highest possible. The Kodokan never did. With her own school, teaching in many countries, writing books, hosting championships, and founding a judo scholarship fund, Keiko generously advanced the art of judo.

Barrier-Breaking Tennis Champion

Althea Gibson
(1927-2003)

The daughter of cotton farm workers, Althea Gibson's life began in South Carolina, United States. When she was three years old, her family moved to the Harlem area of New York City. They were poor, but Althea found escape in sports. An athletic girl, she showed natural talent for tennis. By the time she was eighteen, she won ten straight tournaments sponsored by the American Tennis Association, an organization founded by black tennis players. This helped her get a college athletic scholarship. In college, Althea played in tournaments around the United States. At twenty-three, she made her debut in the national tournament, the US Open, and just barely lost. But it was a big deal because tennis was a white-dominated sport then, and she was the first black person to compete in this championship. Althea also broke major barriers when she became the first black player to win the singles competition in the French Open, Wimbledon, and the US Open. She broke even more barriers when she ultimately won eleven Grand Slam tournaments, which is winning the Australian Open, French Open, Wimbledon, and the US Open all in one year. By age thirty-one, Althea was ranked the number one women's tennis player in the world! She was also great at golf and became the first black to compete on the women's professional golf tour. Althea was inducted into nine halls of fame and was the first black person to be on the cover of *Time* magazine and *Sports Illustrated*. She is on *Sports Illustrated's* 1900-2000 list of the Top 100 Female Athletes. Althea has been a major inspiration to many women and minority players that followed her and will always remain one of tennis' shining icons.

One of the Greatest Romanian Olympians

Lia Manoliu
(1932-1998)

Born in what is now Moldova, Romania, Lia Manoliu came from a family that valued intellect and learning. Her father was a philosophy professor and made sure she got an excellent education, including fluency in four foreign languages. Lia also liked sports. In her teens, she played ping-pong, tennis, volleyball, and basketball and was in national competitions. At sixteen years old, she started throwing the discus. At age eighteen, Lia became the first Romanian woman to throw the discus over 131 feet. She got a college degree in electrical engineering and worked in this field until her athletic career took over. At age twenty, Lia competed in her first Olympics, finishing sixth. She trained hard, sometimes jumping with 300 pounds on her back. In 1960, she was a discus bronze medalist and in 1964 won another bronze. At age thirty-five, the Romanian Athletics Federation told Lia she was too old to train for another Olympics. This only made her more determined, and after months of training herself, she qualified for the Mexico City Olympics. Her discus throw was 190 feet, 2 inches and won her the gold medal. This made Lia the oldest woman to win an Olympic title in track and field. She made her longest discus throw of over 203 feet and 7 inches at age forty! During her athletic career, Lia also competed in championships in her home country as well as European and Balkan Games championships. In her forties, Lia served as vice president and president of the Romanian Olympic Committee. Later, she even got into politics and was elected to the Romanian Senate in the early 1990s. Lia will always be remembered as one of the greatest discus throwers in history.

Record-Setting Sprinter

Betty Cuthbert
(1938-2017)

Betty Cuthbert was from New South Wales, Australia. She started running at the young age of eight and was trained by her physical education teacher. At just thirteen years old, she won a gold medal at Australia's national track and field championships for school sports. Her family owned a nursery, and at age sixteen she left high school to work there. And she trained. At age eighteen, Betty set out to qualify for the Olympic Games, which were being held in her country. She qualified—more than qualified. She won and set new records in the 100 and 200-meter sprinting races. Betty also helped set a record in the 4 x 100-meter relay race, where four team members each run 100 meters, then pass a baton to the next. Betty ran fourth, as what is called the "anchor," and the fastest person on the team. Winning gold medals in these events, she became a national heroine. At age twenty-four, Betty was on the Australian relay team that won a gold medal at the British Empire and Commonwealth Games. Two years later, Betty got her fourth gold medal in the 400-meter race. She remains the only Olympic sprinter to have won gold medals in the 100, 200, and 400-meter races. Betty won many awards, and there is a famous sculpture of her at the sports stadium called Sydney Cricket Ground. Sadly, in her early forties, she was diagnosed with multiple sclerosis. She became a passionate campaigner for research and awareness of this disease. In 2000, in a wheelchair, she was one of the bearers of the Olympic Torch at the Summer Olympic Games. Betty is remembered as the "Golden Girl" of Australia for her sporting contributions.

Warrior Women

South American
Revolutionary War Heroine

Manuela Saenz
(1797-1856)

Manuela Saenz was born in Quito, Ecuador, to a Spanish nobleman and a wealthy Ecuadorian mother. Growing up she was educated at a convent and while living at her mother's family ranch. At the ranch Manuela got exposed to how many people in regions of her country wanted liberation from Spain, which ruled at that time. By age twenty, her father had arranged for her to marry a wealthy Englishman twice her age. They moved to Lima, Peru, where she lived a wealthy woman's life, entertaining political and military elites as guests. Her interest in revolutionary politics deepened, and she began holding political meetings at their home. Manuela and female friends organized women to raise money for revolution needs, such as ships and uniforms. At age twenty-five she left her husband. She met Simón Bolívar, the leader of the revolution from Spanish rule. They became romantically involved, and she became his chief confidante and advisor. Manuela did not conform to traditional feminine behavior at the time; she smoked, swore, wore red pants and a black poncho, had excellent horseback riding skills, and was trained for military action. Manuela went into combat with Bolívar, and in 1828, saved him from assassination. He began calling her the "Liberator of the Liberator." When Bolívar died, the new political and military leader exiled her. She continued to speak out even in exile. In her active revolutionary years, she received the highest civil and military award given by Peru, called the Order of the Sun. There are books and films about her, and there is a museum in Quito in her honor. Manuela bravely pushed the boundaries of what a woman could accomplish during 19th century revolutionary times in South America.

BUFFALO SOLDIER

First Black Female
to Serve in the Army

Cathay Williams
(1844-circa 1893)

Born into slavery in Missouri, United States, Cathay Williams worked as a domestic slave for a wealthy plantation owner. When the Civil War started, the Union forces (who wanted the abolishment of slavery) made former slaves serve in military support roles and paid them. In her late teens, Cathay traveled with and did domestic work for a colonel, a general, and their staff and saw what military life was like. When the war was over, Cathay wanted to keep her financial independence, but there were no post-war jobs for freed slaves. Many of them went into the military for a job, education, healthcare, and pension benefits. Cathay decided to do the same. The problem: women were not allowed in the armed forces. So at 5'9", tall for a woman, she dressed in men's clothing, reversed her name to William Cathay, and enlisted in the Army. The Army did not require full medical exams then, and she passed as fit for duty. At age twenty-two, Cathay became the first documented black woman to serve in the U.S. Army disguised as a man! She served in one of the Army's all-black infantry regiments called Buffalo Soldiers. At age twenty-four Cathay got sick, the doctor found out she was a woman, and she was honorably discharged. Eight years later, a reporter published her amazing story in *The St. Louis Daily Times*. In her late forties, she applied for a disability pension due to health issues. The exact date of her death is unknown, but is believed it was shortly after being denied pension because her Army service was technically not legal. We do know that Cathay was a courageous example of what a woman could do for herself and her country.

REVOLUTIONARY LEGEND

Radical Russian Revolutionary

Vera Figner
(1852-1942)

Of noble German and Russian descent, Vera Figner started life in Kazan Governorate, Russian Empire. As a girl, she received traditional education for wealthy girls at the time but had a mind of her own. Vera pursued history and literature and read books girls were forbidden to read. After graduating with a top academic prize, Vera wanted to pursue a degree that would help the people of her country and chose medicine. Women were not allowed to study medicine in Russia then, so she went to the University of Zurich in Switzerland. While there she joined a group of Russian women, who would become leading women in Russian political movements to come. Her time with this group was transformative. Vera's identity changed from a woman of privilege to an activist wanting social, political, and economic change in Russia. At age twenty-four, she graduated from medical school and began working in peasant villages, seeing their realities firsthand. Four years later, Vera joined the revolutionary People's Will Party. The Party demanded representative government, free press, free speech, and free elections. Without it, the Party called for overthrowing the government and the execution of Tsar Alexander II for crimes committed against the people of the Russian Empire. At age twenty-eight, Vera had become a leader in the Party and played a significant support role in the Tsar's assassination. Two years later, she was captured and imprisoned. After over twenty years in a brutal prison environment, Vera was released. She published *Memoirs of a Revolutionist*, which made her famous. Vera also wrote biographies of activists and articles on the Russian revolutionary movement from the 1870s-1880s. Vera goes down in history as a dedicated revolutionary who was willing to go to radical lengths for the betterment of her country.

The First Female in the Marine Corps

Opha May Johnson
(1878-1955)

Opha May Johnson was from Indiana, United States, and was raised in Washington, D.C. At age seventeen, she graduated as salutatorian of her class (second highest to valedictorian) in shorthand and typewriting from Wood's Commercial College in Washington, D.C. Opha worked in administrative jobs for the federal government until 1918. World War I had been going on for four years, and the Marine Corps needed to fill administrative jobs in the United States vacated by men fighting overseas. The Marine Corps invited women to enlist. On the first recruiting day at the Washington, D.C. Marine Reserve recruiting station, Opha was the first woman in a long line of women there wanting to enlist. Thousands of women showed up for recruiting day in other major cities. In addition to excellent administrative skills, the Marines required strong mental and physical stamina. Only a small portion of the women were successfully enlisted. At age thirty-nine, Opha was one of them. And because she had been first in line, she became the first woman to join the United States Marine Corps Women's Reserve. The women trained and drilled like other Marines, and it was tough. They were also paid the same as the male members of the Corps. Opha was first assigned to the Marine headquarters in Arlington, Virginia. She got promoted to Sergeant and became the highest-ranking woman in the Marine Corps at the time. When the war ended in 1919, so did her military service. After leaving the Marines, Opha remained a strong advocate for women in the military. Although her time of service was short, Opha's contribution to Marine Corps history is significant. Being the first female in the Marine Corps broke barriers and, with hundreds like her, paved the way for women in the military.

Fearless Fighter for Mother Russia

Maria Bochkareva
(1889-1920)

Maria Bochkareva was born into a poor family in Kirillovsky Uyezd, Russia. She had an abusive father, and at just fifteen years old got married to get away from him. By age twenty-four, two troublesome marriages had ended, and World War I had started. Maria decided to change her life and join the war effort. Women had to get permission from the leader of Russia at the time. Semiliterate, a military officer helped her write the leader requesting permission. It was granted, and after three months of training, Maria was sent to frontline duty on the Russian-German front. She had to prove her courage in battle to the men in the unit, which she did. She bravely fought, got injured, rehabilitated, and returned to the front lines. She won several medals between 1915-1917. When male soldier morale problems started, it was decided to create the first all-female battalion. Maria was selected to lead it, becoming the first Russian woman to command a military unit. The women wore men's uniforms, and they shaved their heads just like the men. The battalion was called the Battalion of Death because they were willing to fight to death to protect their Mother Russia. When it came time to fight, the male soldiers did not support them. The Battalion of Death went to the front lines anyway and took out lines of German enemies. But the success of the battalion did not last. A revolution was also looming inside Russia. The communist Bolshevik party had seized power, and she was seen as an anti-revolutionary. Maria left Russia and met with political leaders, even the U.S. President, begging them to intervene. Maria returned to Russia to join anti-Bolshevik forces. At age thirty, her fight ended. The Bolsheviks captured and executed this fearless and dedicated fighter.

Sister Heroine of the Holocaust

Ida Cook
(1904-1986)

Beginning her life in County Durham, England, Ida Cook completed high school, then worked in governmental service. She also became a romance novelist. Ida's story can't be told without her older sister, Louise (who had no children either). In the 1930s, they lived together, shared a love of opera, and traveled to other countries to see performances. They regularly went to Germany and Austria. Through an Austrian conductor and his opera vocalist wife, the sisters learned about the horrors of Nazi treatment of the Jews. They decided to do something about it. Their visits to Germany to see opera became a cover operation for rescuing the Jews from the Nazis. The British government allowed very few Jewish refugees, and they had to prove they had money to live on. Fleeing for their lives made this difficult. To help them, Ida and Louise devised a plan. Every time Ida and Louise left Germany, they smuggled refugees' valuables like furs and jewelry by wearing them over their plain clothes. It was dangerous; if they were questioned by bodyguards, their lives could be at risk. Once in Britain, the refugees could sell their valuables to live on. Ida and Louise also helped the refugees forge documents and gave them a small apartment to live in. While Ida had done well with her book sales, some people don't believe it was enough to finance the rescue efforts and suspect that the sisters were also spies for the British government. This has never been proven. Ida, the more outgoing of the two sisters, gave speeches all over England to raise money for refugee Jews. Books tell Ida and Louise's story, and they were honored by the British government and the World Holocaust Remembrance Center as heroes of the Holocaust.

OUTSMARTING NAZI REGIME

The Fearless White Mouse

Nancy Wake
(1912-2011)

Two years after being born in the Wellington region of New Zealand, Nancy Wake and her family moved to Australia. At age sixteen, she left home and did nursing work to save money. With financial help from her aunt, she went to Europe. In London, she learned how to become a journalist. In her early twenties, she got a job working as a correspondent for *The Chicago Tribune* in Paris and reported on the rise of the Nazis. On assignment in Austria, she saw the Jews getting beaten by Nazi gangs and committed to do what she could to stop the Nazis. Nancy joined a group called The Resistance. When Hitler's forces invaded France, she started doing undercover work to help local Resistance groups and get British soldiers and refugees out of France to safety. Nancy helped save the lives of hundreds of soldiers and downed airmen between 1940-1943. She was so good at not getting captured the Nazi secret police started calling her "the white mouse." When Nancy got to the top of their most wanted list she hid in the back of a coal truck and escaped to France. Then she joined the Special Operations Executive (SOE), an intelligence group working with the French Resistance. After intense training, she was part of over 450 SOEs who parachuted into France to help arm and lead resistance fighters. "I was never afraid," she said. "I was too busy to be afraid." After the war and the Nazis were defeated, Nancy received many awards for her wartime bravery. Her book, *The White Mouse*, is about her adventures, and there are biographies and television shows about her. This fearless fighter died at age ninety-nine, her ashes spread over where she fought in a heroic attack on a Nazi headquarters.

Making Military Nursing History

Hazel Johnson-Brown
(1927-2011)

Hazel Johnson-Brown was born into a farming family in Pennsylvania, United States. Everyone in her family worked the farm and had other jobs. At age twelve, Hazel also did domestic work outside the home. At this age, she already knew she wanted to be a nurse. After graduating high school, Hazel applied to nursing school in Pennsylvania but was rejected because she was black. This was not uncommon at the time. She moved to New York and went to Harlem School of Nursing, a school specifically for black women. After graduating at age twenty-three, she worked in the Harlem Hospital emergency ward, then for a Veterans Administration hospital. There she learned about opportunities in the Army Nurse Corps, which was now racially integrated, and was inspired to enlist. She served from the age of twenty-eight into her mid-fifties. Hazel took combat military nursing assignments in South Korea, Japan, and trained nurses for service in Vietnam. She rose in the ranks while she earned her bachelor's degree in nursing, master's degree in nursing education, and Ph.D. in educational administration. At age fifty-two, Hazel made history by becoming the highest-ranking black woman in the armed services. She was promoted to the rank of general in the U.S. Army and the first black chief of the Army Nurse Corps. She oversaw over 200 army healthcare facilities around the world and commanded about 7,000 military nurses. She had many military decorations, including the Army Distinguished Service Medal, Meritorious Service Medal, and Army Commendation Medal. Twice she was named nurse of the year. After the Army, she became a university professor. When she died, the U.S. House of Representatives passed a Joint Resolution commending Hazel's outstanding military nursing contributions and dedication to the U.S. Army.

Lovers & Explorers
of the Natural World

Bold Traveler & Treasure Seeker

Hester Stanhope
(1776-1839)

Hester Stanhope was born into a British aristocratic family in Kent, England. Her mother died when she was young and her father remarried, adding three younger half-brothers, with whom she would become very close. She was educated by governesses and her father, who also encouraged her love of horseback riding, which would serve her greatly later in life. In her late teens, she went to live with her uncle, who was the Prime Minister. After one of the brothers was killed in war and her uncle died when she was twenty years old, she decided to hit the road with no destination. Inspired to explore, she traveled for over two years to Greece, present-day Istanbul, Malta, Palestine, Lebanon, and Syria. In Malta, she was in a shipwreck, survived, but lost all her clothes. Not afraid to be unconventional, Hester started wearing men's local clothing, even wearing a turban. Knowing she might encounter hostile nomadic tribes, with her entourage (including twenty-two camels) Hester dangerously traveled through the desert to the city of Palmyra, Syria. She learned of a medieval scroll that described a hidden treasure under the ruins of a mosque in the city of Ashkelon. Hester decided she would try to find this treasure. She persuaded local authorities to allow her to excavate this site. While she or no one had done this before, Hester led a thorough and well-recorded archeological excavation. Although she didn't find the treasure, Hester became an archaeological pioneer. After she died, memoirs of her adventures were published. There are two movies based on her life, *Harem* and *Queen of the East*. Hester's bold Middle Eastern explorations brought her the name, 'Queen of the Desert' and her groundbreaking archeological dig influenced archeologists to come.

The Force Behind Modern Birdwatching

Florence Bailey
(1863-1948)

From an early age, Florence Bailey explored her natural environment in the northeastern part of New York, United States, where she was born. Growing up, she loved the wildlife on her family's estate and in the Adirondack Mountains near her home. Florence attended private school and was very educated by the age of eleven. She attended Smith College in Massachusetts, and by her final year, was passionate about ornithology, the study of birds. Florence wrote a series of articles for *Audubon Magazine*, and at twenty-six years old, published them in her first book, *Birds Through an Opera Glass*. Unlike previous works that studied birds trapped in indoor settings, she was the first to advocate studying them using binoculars in their natural habitat. This approach would come to define modern-day birdwatching. Florence went on to publish over fifty articles in ornithology journals and nine birdwatching field guides designed for the public. Florence was dead-set against the use of bird feathers in the hat-making industry and worked to pass the Lacey Act of 1900, which prohibits the trade of illegally acquired wildlife and the federal Migratory Bird Treaty Act of 1918, which made the protection of migratory birds a federal law. She also worked to introduce nature study into school curriculum and taught birding courses for the public. Florence was elected the first woman Fellow in the American Ornithologists' Union and the first woman to be awarded the Brewster Medal for her exceptional body of ornithology work. At age seventy, the University of Mexico awarded her an honorary doctorate. A bird expert like no other, Florence inspired the love of birdwatching for the masses and was a major force behind it becoming a popular hobby.

First Mexican-American Woman Botanist

Ynes Mexia
(1870-1938)

Ynez Mexia's life began in Washington, D.C., United States. Her parents divorced when she was very young. Her father returned to his native Mexico, and she moved to Texas with her mother. A quiet child who liked to be alone, Ynez loved to explore the outdoors. In her twenties, when her father was dying, he asked her to take over his ranch in Mexico, which she did. Ynez learned to manage the ranch well, but her second husband tragically bankrupted it, which devastated her. She divorced him and wanted a fresh start. After thirty years in Mexico, she moved to San Francisco, California. She joined the Sierra Club and Save the Redwoods League and became very active in saving forests. At age fifty-one, Ynez began taking classes at the University of California Berkeley and found she loved botany, the study of plants. As part of a flowering plant course, she went on her first expedition to Mexico. Her love of solitude led her to leave the research group to collect specimens on her own. Ynez traveled by herself in Mexico for two years and collected more than 1,500 plant specimens. For the next thirteen years, she would go to many areas in North and South America that had not been explored by botanists before. She gained the reputation of being the first Mexican-American botanist. On one of her most adventurous trips, she canoed 3,000 miles on the Amazon River. Ynez ended up collecting over 145,000 plant specimens and became the most accomplished female botanical collector of her time. When she died, Ynez left much of her estate to where it all started, the Sierra Club and Save the Redwoods League.

Gutsy Arctic Explorer

Louise Arner Boyd
(1887-1972)

Louise Arner Boyd was born in California, United States, and had a father who struck it rich as a gold miner. Louise went to very good schools, was a tomboy, and liked horseback riding and hunting with her two older brothers. Even as a child, she was fascinated by stories of people exploring the Arctic. Her brothers died when she was a teenager, and both of her parents had passed away by the time she was thirty-two years old. With her generous inheritance, she decided to follow her dream to go to the Arctic. Between 1926 and 1941, Louise went on seven expeditions to the Arctic. To prepare, she intensely studied all types of geology, biology, and learned photography. Although she did not have a degree, she held her own with the all-male crews she hired who were experienced with dangerous Arctic scientific expeditions. A huge amount of data was gathered in her expeditions that are still used by scientists today. In her forties, Louise also went on a special mission to find a famous Arctic explorer who had disappeared. He was not found, but Louise won awards from the Norwegian and French governments for her courageous efforts. Having gained respectable expertise, during World War I the military hired Louise as a consultant on Arctic-related military matters. Gusty from the start, on all her expeditions, Louise had tireless energy, determination, and perseverance. She even loved the extreme cold weather! She received awards for her great work, and at sixty-eight years old, became the first woman to fly over the North Pole. Louise spent her entire fortune on polar science research, and when she died, had her ashes scattered over the place she loved, the Arctic.

A Legend for the Lions

Joy Adamson
(1910-1980)

Joy Adamson was from what is now the Moravian-Silesian Region of the northeastern Czech Republic. Hunting was a favorite sport on the family's property. As a teenager she shot a deer, hated it, and promised herself she would never kill for sport again. At age twenty-eight Joy married a botanist (one who studies plants). She traveled to Kenya with him and published seven hundred of their plant findings. By her mid-thirties, she had divorced and married a game warden in Kenya. In 1956, he shot a female lion in self-defense but learned after that it had only attacked to protect her three cubs. He rescued the young animals and brought them home to Joy. They found it hard to care for the needs of all three of them, so gave two away to a zoo, but kept one. They named it Elsa, and Joy developed a close bond with it. In her bestselling book *Born Free: A Lioness of Two Worlds*, she tells the story of her relationship with Elsa and her efforts to return her to the wild. She then wrote *Living Free: The Story of Elsa and Her Cubs,* and *Forever Free: Elsa's Pride*. Joy's story and fascinating writings inspired the animal conservation movement in Africa. *Born Free* became an Academy Award-winning film and a famous song. Her books also include *The Peoples of Kenya* and *Queen of Shaba: The Story of an African Leopard*. In her fifties and sixties, Joy did speaking tours around the world on wildlife preservation, founded nonprofit preservation organizations, and funded animal reserves. After over forty years of wildlife preservation work in Africa, Joy met a tragic death: she was stabbed to death by a former employee. But her legendary work lives on.

Passionate Protector of Primates

Dian Fossey
(1932-1985)

A lover of animals from an early age, Dian Fossey was born in California, United States. After graduating college, she worked with children as an occupational therapist. At age thirty-one, Dian was ready for an adventure and used all her savings and borrowed money to pay for a trip to Africa. This would change her life forever. In Africa, she befriended Joan and Alan Root, wildlife photographers who were working on a documentary of African gorillas. She also met Mary Leakey, a well-known paleoanthropologist (one who studies human evolution through archeology) and Louis Leakey, an archaeologist. All of them influenced Dian's developing passion for studying primates. The Leakeys helped her get funding to study gorillas. For twenty years, she passionately studied and defended endangered gorillas in Rwanda. Dian felt her earlier work with children helped her have the skill to gain the trust of the mountain gorillas. She also got a Ph.D. in zoology. Dian fiercely went after poachers who bribed park rangers into letting them trap and kill gorillas. It is believed that Dian's efforts to defend the gorillas is what led to her murder at age fifty-three. Was it a research assistant she had fired, or the gorilla tracker with whom she worked? Rwanda's ruling class because Dian knew too much about illegal gorilla trafficking at the highest levels? Or because she was against gorilla-related tourism? While still a mystery, we do know that Dian became one of the world's leading experts on mountain gorillas and made an amazing contribution to the understanding of these amazing animals. We have her story in her book, *Gorillas in the Mist*, which is also a famous movie. Dian's spirit of protection also lives on with her fund, the Dian Fossey Gorilla Fund International.

Legendary Lenswomen

Pioneering Science Photographer

Anna Atkins
(1799-1871)

With the birth name of Anna Children, Anna Atkins was from Kent, England. Her father, John Children was a respected chemist, mineralogist, and zoologist. Her mother died early in her life when Anna was only a year old. As a girl, she became interested in science and botany, the study of plants. In 19th century Victorian England, a time when women were not allowed to be professional scientists, because of her father, Anna was fortunate to study science. She loved botany and would spend most of her adult life studying it. Anna came to know how difficult it was to make accurate illustrations of plants and wanted to find a way to get pictures of the plants themselves. Through her father and husband, Pelly Atkins, she met a known astronomer and chemist, Sir John Herschel, and she found her answer. He had developed the photographic process called cyanotyping, and she used it to develop her book, *Photographs of British Algae: Cyanotype Impressions*. It presented all of the kinds of algae found in the British Isles and was the first book to ever be illustrated with photographs. She would publish twelve more editions of this book and with her friend Anne Dixon use the same process to publish albums of flowering plants and ferns. Anna produced thousands of botanical illustrations using cyanotyping, many of which are in museums and private collections. While in time, newer ways of photographing for scientific purposes developed, Anna's work remains widely collected and admired. Today her botanical illustrations are sold as art. In 2018, the New York Public Library had an exhibition on Anna's life and work. She was a true pioneer in showing how photography can be artfully used in science.

Master Photojournalist

Margaret Bourke-White
(1904-1971)

Margaret White started life in New York, United States. When she was young, she wanted to grow up and become a herpetologist, one who studies reptiles and amphibians. At seventeen years old, she went to Columbia University to do just that. There she also took photography and liked it so much, it became a hobby. Although Margaret then studied zoology at the University of Michigan and graduated from Cornell University with a degree in biology, she decided to become a photographer. She combined her own last name with her mother's maiden name (Bourke) to create her hyphenated professional name. Margaret moved to Cleveland, Ohio, started doing photographs for industry and architectural firms, and quickly gained a reputation. At age twenty-five, a new magazine called *Fortune* hired her, and her career took off. Margaret moved to New York and had many photojournalism assignments around the world. For *Fortune* and then *LIFE* magazines, she took photos of industrialization in Russia, people during the Depression in the United States, and many aspects of World War II in Europe and Russia. She was the first woman to go with air crews on bombing missions during war and traveled with the U.S. army as it freed concentration camps in Germany. Margaret's photographs of people in the camps and corpses in gas chambers shocked the world. She interviewed and photographed Mohandas Gandhi, the leader of India's nonviolent independence movement, and covered unrest in South Africa and the Korean War. She blazed the trail for photojournalism and photo essays of major world events and published eleven books. One of the most respected photojournalists of her time, in 1935, Margaret was named one of the twenty most notable American women.

LIFE Magazine's
First Female Photographer

Nina Leen
(1914?-1995)

Nina Leen was born in Russia, but we aren't sure of the year. Her whole life she kept her age a secret. A bit of a nomad in her young adult life, Nina studied art in Germany, lived in France, Switzerland, and Italy before coming to the United States in what is estimated as her early to mid-twenties. Her first camera was a German "Rolleiflex," a twin-lens camera that used film, and with it she taught herself how to take pictures. Nina was only in the United States for a year before *LIFE* magazine, a famous magazine that chronicled the 20th century in photo essays, published her shots of fighting tortoises at the Bronx Zoo in New York. Nina would go on to publish photos for *LIFE* for thirty years, including over fifty covers and many photo essays from places around the world. She was known for her pictures of animals, humans with animals, teenagers in the 1940s and 1950s, and fashion. From farmers in the Ozark mountains in the United States to abstract artists, Nina also did a wide range of group portraits that became famous. No matter what she shot, Nina was known for her ability to photograph everyday people and scenes and capture the feelings and real story. In addition to her work for *LIFE*, Nina published fifteen photo books, one of which was on bats, which she loved. When Nina died, a press agent for *LIFE* magazine was reported to have guessed she was in her late 70s or early 80s, but her exact age remained unknown. We do know she left behind quite the legacy of photography.

Brilliant Street Photographer

Vivian Maier
(1926-2009)

Vivian Maier had an Austrian father and French mother, and was born in New York, United States. She spent her youth moving between France and the United States. Part of this time she and her mother lived with an award-winning photographer, Jeanne Bertrand. Vivian began taking photos herself in her early twenties, and at thirty years old, she moved to Chicago, Illinois, where she would live the rest of her life. For many years, Vivian worked as a live-in caregiver while doing street photography on the side. Shooting in black and white, she was drawn to taking photos of the less fortunate on the streets of Chicago and captured interesting, strange, and touching situations. Later Vivian started shooting in color with an abstract approach with more objects than people. Free-spirited and curious, in her early thirties, she traveled solo internationally, always with her camera. During her life, Vivian's amazing pictures were never seen by the public. Being a private person, she chose to keep her photography private as well. In tough financial times, her work was put in storage. After her death, three men ended up buying Vivian's photos, prints, film rolls, and negatives at auction and saw the brilliance of her work. One of them, John Maloof, became passionately driven to make her work known, organized exhibitions, wrote books, and became one of the directors of the documentary about her called *Finding Vivian Maier*, which was nominated for an Oscar in 2015. Another buyer, Jeff Goldstein, produced exhibitions of her work as well. Thanks to these efforts since her death, we can only hope that Vivian is somewhere out there hopefully filled with pride that her brilliant street photography is now a public legacy.

Documentary Photographer
for the Fringes

Mary Ellen Mark
(1940-2015)

Mary Ellen Mark was born in Pennsylvania, United States, and from an early age loved to paint and draw. When she was nine years old, she got her first camera. Mary Ellen received a bachelor's degree in painting and art history, a master's degree in photojournalism, and later in her life five honorary doctorate degrees in fine arts. In her late twenties, Mary Ellen moved to New York and got photography work for well-respected magazines, including *Look*, *Time*, *The New York Times Magazine*, and *Rolling Stone*. Mostly shooting in black and white, she did documentary photography, which focuses on capturing the world as it is. Mary Ellen's work makes us look at troubling social issues like mental illness, drug addiction, prostitution, and homelessness. In her words, "I feel an affinity for people who haven't had the best breaks in society. What I want to do more than anything is acknowledge their existence." Mary Ellen had a natural ability to develop relationships with her subjects. On one project, for several weeks she lived with women in a maximum-security ward of a state mental hospital in Oregon. On another, she spent three months making friends with and taking pictures of prostitutes who worked on just one street in Bombay, India. Mary Ellen's famous series of photos of street kids in Seattle, Washington, who were panhandlers, prostitutes, and drug dealers was made into a documentary film called *Streetwise* which was nominated for an Academy Award in 1984. Mary Ellen's work has been exhibited around the world. She published twenty books and received over thirty awards for photographic excellence. With objectivity and compassion, Mary Ellen's important work shows us much about the pained lives of those who live on the tough fringes of society.

Daring War Photographer

Catherine Leroy
(1944-2006)

From the suburbs of Paris, France, growing up Catherine Leroy wanted to be a classical pianist. But her life would turn out differently. At age eighteen, Catherine got a parachutist license, which was rare for women at the time. She loved the French newspaper, *Paris Match*, and at age twenty-one, was so moved by images of the Vietnam war, she decided to go there herself. She booked a one-way ticket to the country of Laos and left with a camera and about two hundred dollars in her pocket. At a time when women were rarely war photographers, Catherine approached the news organization, the Associated Press, to see if she could take photographs for them. When asked if she had any experience, she lied and said she did. She was given a chance, and did she deliver. During the next three years, often in danger, she shot many powerful pictures that were published in the world's most famous magazines. Having a parachutist license also gave Catherine the chance to be the only non-military photographer and only woman to parachute jump in combat. She covered conflicts in Lebanon, Northern Ireland, Cyprus, Somalia, Afghanistan, Iraq, Iran, and Libya, and became internationally famous. Catherine received many awards and published the books, *Under Fire: Great Photographers and Writers in Vietnam* and *God Cried*, showing the pain and suffering in the Lebanon war. There is a book about her, *Close Up On War: The Story of Pioneering Photojournalist Catherine Leroy in Vietnam*, and a documentary about her called *Cathy at War*. From her daring move as a young woman to fly to a war zone to bravely covering many international conflicts, Catherine became one of the most accomplished war photographers of her generation.

Fiery Informers

Challenging Big Business

Ida Tarbell
(1857-1944)

Born in Pennsylvania, United States, Ida Tarbell became a famous investigative journalist who took on big business. When she was a teen, she saw how her father, a small oil producer, was the victim of what is called the Oil War of 1872. He and other small oil producers were forced to sell their businesses to Standard Oil Company or go out of business. Little did Ida know then that years later she would shine a bright light on this huge company's unfair business practices. After finishing college, she briefly worked as a teacher. At age twenty-six, she took a job at a local magazine. This is when she became passionate about writing about the social problems of the day. When Ida was thirty-four, she made a bold move and went to live in Paris. She went to Sorbonne University, one of the most respected universities in Europe and the world. While studying there she made money by writing articles for American magazines. Three years later, she got a job at *McClure* magazine. There Ida wrote a nineteen-part series on Standard Oil Company's monopoly, which are unethical business practices that drive competitors out of business. In 1904, her amazing work became a successful book titled, *The History of the Standard Oil Company*, which New York University put as number five on a list of the top 100 works of 20th-century American journalism. Ida's investigation is credited to have led to the 1911 ruling by the U.S. Supreme Court that broke up the company's monopoly. In her sixties, Ida was still writing, including her autobiography titled, *All in the Day's Work*. Ida's contributions to investigative journalism took it to new levels for the benefit of political, economic, and industrial change.

Daring Undercover Reporter (& World Record Holder!)

Nellie Bly
(1864-1922)

Nellie Bly was not her given name; it was Elizabeth Cochran. Her father, Michael Cochran, a judge and landowner, founded the town she was born in, Cochran's Mills, Pennsylvania. When she was eighteen, she wrote a heated response to an article in the *Pittsburgh Dispatch* newspaper that criticized women who worked outside the home. It got the attention of the newspaper's managing editor who offered her a starting position. When Elizabeth was twenty-three, her boss challenged her to investigate problems at a mental hospital on Blackwell's Island, New York. She took on a fake name, Nellie Brown, and pretended to be mentally ill to get admitted and stayed there ten days. What she learned became a famous six-part exposé about bad conditions, neglect, and physical abuse at this mental hospital. Nellie's reporting led to a large investigation and much-needed improvements in patient care. She continued her exposé work in New York jails, factories, employment agencies, and political corruption. Nellie became known for taking on issues that would contribute to the betterment of society, writing with a strong voice and detail. She was the top journalist of her day, and her success led newspapers to hire more women. If this was not enough, at twenty-five Nellie also became famous for setting a world record. She read Jules Verne's novel, *Around the World in 80 Days*, and decided she wanted to beat this fictional record. And she did; she finished the trip in seventy-two days. Her book, *Around the World in Seventy-Two Days*, was a huge success. In her later years, Nellie continued worthy reporting work, and when she died, the *New York Evening Journal* remembered her as "the best reporter in America."

Fighter for Mexican-American Civil Rights

Jovita Idar
(1885-1946)

Jovita Idar was born and raised in Laredo, Texas, which is on the border between the United States and Mexico. Her father was a known community leader and civil rights activist and ran the family newspaper called *La Crónica*. It was a time when racial segregation not only affected blacks, but Mexican Americans as well. As a young woman, she started working as a reporter for this newspaper. Jovita wrote about segregation issues and took on fake pen names, including Astraea, the Greek goddess of justice, and Ave Negra, Spanish for black bird. Jovita also wrote about equal rights for women and promoted their education and independence from men. And after being exposed to lynchings of Mexican-American men, she became even more committed to Mexican-American civil rights. In her mid-twenties, Jovita's family organized a convention called the First Mexican Congress, which started the modern Mexican-American civil rights movement. After this, Jovita helped create and was president of one of the first Latina feminist organizations called the League of Mexican Women. When Jovita was working at the *El Progreso* newspaper, she wrote an article protesting the current president's, Woodrow Wilson, decision to send U.S. troops to the border. When the U.S. Army and border security officials came to *El Progreso*'s doors, Jovita stood her ground and did not let them in. The paper was ultimately forced to shut down, but not without a fight by Jovita. After the Mexican Revolution during which she worked as a nurse, she started her own newspaper called *Evolución*. Later, she worked as a translator, teacher, and helped undocumented workers get their naturalization papers. As a journalist, activist, and teacher, Jovita devoted her life to the equal rights and education of Mexican Americans.

Tireless Challenger of Racial Discrimination

Claudia Jones
(1915-1964)

Claudia Jones' given name was Claudia Vera Cumberbatch. She was from Port of Spain, Trinidad, in the West Indies. When she was seven years old, she and her family moved to Harlem in New York City. They were poor, and she saw how badly blacks and working-class people were treated. As a young woman, she learned of a court case called the Scottsboro case that would change her life. Nine young African American men were wrongfully accused of raping two white girls, and she became aware that Communist Party USA was very involved in seeing that the boys got the fair treatment and justice they deserved. At the time, Communists were active in promoting civil rights and racial equality for blacks, which inspired Claudia to join the Young Communist League. She would spend the rest of her life as a member of Communist Party USA, which was not easy. Claudia changed her last name to "Jones" to avoid harassment from those who opposed her political beliefs. For years she tirelessly wrote and spoke out about human rights issues and the social change needed to create equitable societies. She was jailed for her "un-American" activities with Communist Party USA, the Party that gave her legal assistance and got her out on bail. The last time she was jailed she lost the court case and was deported to England. This did not stop her, though. In her mid-forties, Claudia started the *West Indian Gazette*, one of the first major black newspapers in England, which allowed her to continue to challenge racism in housing, education, and employment. When Claudia died, many people around the world including Martin Luther King Jr. sent condolences to Claudia, whose life was boldly lived.

Cosmopolitan's Queen & More

Helen Gurley Brown
(1922-2012)

Born in Arkansas, United States, Helen Gurley Brown grew up during the Depression. She and her family moved to California when she was a teen. At nineteen years old, she got her degree from Woodbury Business College. With typing and shorthand skills, Helen proceeded to have eighteen jobs in seven years before she got hired by an advertising agency called Foote, Cone & Belding. Now in her mid-twenties, at this agency, Helen had a chance to show her copywriting skills. Her career took off. By the time Helen was in her late thirties she had advanced to being one of the nation's highest paid copywriters. When she was forty years old, Helen left advertising when her first book, *Sex and the Single Girl*, became a bestseller. This book gives advice on a range of topics for single women, emphasizes the good things about not being married, encourages women to be financially independent, and not to wait until they are married to have sex lives. To openly discuss that sex is an important part of every woman's single life was radical at the time. Helen went on to write sixteen more books over her career. When she was forty-three years old, she began her career's signature achievement. Helen was hired as the editor-in-chief for *Cosmopolitan* magazine, which was not doing well at the time. She turned it around, attracting young women, single and married. Its flashy cultural, fashion, and lifestyle trendsetting style also pushed the boundaries. In 1972, *Cosmopolitan* boldly published a nude male centerfold. Helen was the editor-in-chief for over thirty years, and under her leadership, *Cosmopolitan* would become one of the most popular and recognized women's magazines around the world.

Journalist Like No Other

Gwen Ifill
(1955-2016)

Gwen Ifill was from New York City, United States. Her father was from Panama and of Barbadian descent, and her mother was from Barbados. As a girl, when she and her family watched news shows, she did not see newscasters or reporters who looked like her. Little did she know then that girls of color would one day be watching *her*! Gwen received a bachelor's degree in communications and got a job at the *Boston Herald*. She went on to work for *The Baltimore Evening Sun* and *The Washington Post* before taking a job at *The New York Times*, covering the White House. At the age of thirty-nine, Gwen got her first job in television, where she was the Capitol Hill reporter for NBC. Five years later, she became the moderator for the show, *Washington Week in Review*, making her the first black woman to moderate a national television political talk show. After also being a senior correspondent on the famous news show, *PBS NewsHour*, Gwen was promoted to co-anchor and co-managing editor for the show. She moderated two vice presidential debates, and in 2016, she and her co-anchor Judy Woodruff were the first women's team to moderate a Democratic presidential debate. In all her roles, Gwen was known for having a unique combination of warmth yet always asking tough questions and passionately defending free press. She published the bestselling book, *The Breakthrough: Politics and Race in the Age of Obama*, and received more than twenty honorary doctorates. Before and after her death, Gwen received many awards for her journalism excellence, including being inducted into the Washington, D.C. Journalism Hall of Fame and the National Association of Black Journalists Hall of Fame.

Fearless Human Rights
Journalist & Activist

Gauri Lankesh
(1962-2017)

Gauri Lankesh was born and grew up in Karnataka, India. Her journalism and activist work started when she was an adult in her thirties. Her father was a known poet and journalist and ran the weekly newspaper called *Lankesh Patrike*. When he died, she was thirty-eight years old, and she and her brother took over the publication. The *Lankesh Patrike* was a voice for the marginalized, lowest classes of people in India. It focused on issues related to people's struggles with discrimination and oppression. Not long after Gauri and her brother took over, they had a falling out, and she started her own weekly publication called *Gauri Lankesh Patrike*. She boldly criticized right-wing Hindu extremism and Hindutva politics, which were against diversity. Gauri campaigned for women's rights and was a strong supporter of the student movement fighting for democracy. In her mid-forties, Gauri published a report on right-wing and Hindu nationalists, and several years later was convicted of defamation, which is the legal term for when someone says something false about a person that then causes that person damage. Gauri spent six months in jail, got out on bail, and appealed the conviction. But the appeal never came; at age fifty-five, she was assassinated because of her outspoken anti-Hindutva activism. After her death, Gauri received the Anna Politkovskaya Award, which is named after the Russian journalist with this name who was murdered as a result of her reporting about the war in Chechnya, Russia. Gauri's gutsy life was also honored in France at the Bayeux-Calvados-Normandy Awards for war correspondents, which recognizes journalists who have worked in dangerous conditions, conflicts, and post-conflict situations to defend freedom and democracy.

Social Changers

ANTI-SLAVERY EQUALITY

Fighting Against Slavery and for Women's Rights

Sarah Grimké
(1792-1873)

Sarah Grimké was born into a well-off family in South Carolina, United States. Her parents gave her private tutors for what girls were supposed to learn in those times, but Sarah wanted to learn what boys were taught in school. Her older brother taught her what he learned in his classes. Her parents were slaveholders, and Sarah saw how they were not allowed to go to school. She began to teach the slaves herself until her father put a stop to it. How slaves were treated and limitations put on her as a female in those times would inspire her courageous activist work for the rest of her life. Sarah wanted to become a lawyer, but back then women could not go to law school. Instead, she and her older sister began speaking in public against slavery and for women's rights. A letter by her sister that was published in an anti-slavery newspaper got a lot of attention and ended up with them being the first women to testify in front of a state legislature on blacks' rights. People protested at their speeches and burned their writings. Even though it got dangerous, it did not stop them. Their audiences grew larger and included men and women, which was highly unusual at the time. In her forties, Sarah published booklets arguing for the end of slavery and women's rights, including *Letters on the Equality of the Sexes and the Condition of Women*. It boldly attacked the idea that women's inferior status was God-given and argued it just reflected the male-dominated society they lived in. In the history books for her lifelong brave work, Sarah showed more courage in the fight for equal rights than most white people in the South at the time.

Pioneer of Housing for the Poor

Octavia Hill
(1838-1912)

Octavia Hill's life began in Cambridgeshire, England. At age two her family experienced financial hardship and had to rely on extended family to get by. When she and her family moved to London, Octavia saw horrible urban poverty. At the age of fourteen, she started working to help poor children make toys to make money for a nonprofit organization serving children in need. Octavia saw firsthand what overcrowded, unsanitary housing and bad nourishment looked like. This experience would set the stage for the rest of her life's work. In her twenties, a friend inherited a good amount of money and three cottages in need of a lot of work. Octavia gave him a proposal: lend her the money to buy the cottages, and she would deliver a five percent profit. He took the chance, and she succeeded in developing an approach to improving and managing the properties that not only gave tenants good quality, well-managed homes, but they turned a profit. Octavia published articles on the terrible living conditions of the poor and how her projects were helping the situation. This drew more investors, including English royalty. Her housing projects grew to other areas of London, and the approach was copied by European countries and the United States. Knowing a lot about the crowded environment of poor people in London also inspired her to work to preserve open spaces. Along with two co-founders, she created the National Trust, which worked to preserve historic and natural places and make them available for all, the wealthy, working class, and the poor, to enjoy. The National Trust still exists today. Octavia created positive social change for how the poor lived, and her pioneering efforts played a role in creating property management as a profession.

One of the First Social Reform Revolutionaries in India

Tarabai Shinde
(1850-1910)

Tarabai Shinde was from an upper-class family in Maharashtra, India. With no girls' schools then, her father homeschooled her. He taught her Marathi, Sanskrit, English, and literature, which was not common for girls at the time. Very independent and self-confident, also unlike most girls, Tarabai rode horses and had good sword skills. Following Indian custom, she married very young. She had more independence than other young Indian wives, however, as her husband came to live with her family, rather than the custom of her living with his. Her passion for social reform started when she became involved with a school for girls in the lower caste, or social class, and a shelter for upper-class widows who were forced into seclusion and forbidden to ever marry again. Her experiences deeply shaped her thinking about oppression of the lower classes and women. In her early thirties, Tarabai's voice became very public due to a well-known case of a young, widowed woman who murdered her newborn child out of fear of being shunned and disgraced. The young woman was sentenced to execution. The case generated much public discussion and articles that criticized Indian women for having "loose morals." Tarabai joined public debates, attacked social and cultural customs, and the mistreatment of women. She published the book, *Stri Purush Tulana*, translated to "A Comparison between Women and Men," which sharply challenged the male-dominated belief that women were inherently inferior to men and smartly analyzed this in a broader context of male-controlled society. Not surprisingly, the book was met with scorn and controversy. But it did something bigger; it made Tarabai a revolutionary force of the time that gave spark to feminist literature and activism in India.

BIRTH
CONTROL
HERO

A Major Financial Force
Behind the Birth Control Pill

Katharine McCormick
(1875-1967)

With ancestors who came to America on the Mayflower, Katharine McCormick was from Michigan, United States. Her father was a known lawyer, and at just fourteen years old, she tragically witnessed him die of a heart attack. Four years later, she lost her brother to a serious infection called meningitis. These losses inspired Katharine to pursue medicine. Her determination got her into the highly regarded Massachusetts Institute of Technology (MIT). At age twenty-nine, she became one of the first women to get a bachelor's degree in biology from MIT and married a wealthy businessman. Shortly after, he was diagnosed with early dementia. For many years she remained committed to his care. During this time, Katharine got involved in the fight for women's right to vote. When that battle was won, in her forties, she began working on getting women contraception. Still illegal, the diaphragm was the best option then. The black market was getting diaphragms into the United States, but not enough of them. Katharine came up with a clever plan. Posing as a scientist, she went to diaphragm manufacturers in Europe, got orders for lots of them, had seamstresses sew them into garments, and had them shipped to the United States. Customs officials just saw the clothes and did not suspect a thing. When her husband died, Katharine inherited a sizable estate. She moved on from the diaphragm scheme and wanted to see the birth control pill be used in her lifetime. She generously used her inheritance to finance the development of and campaign to legalize the pill. She donated $2 million, equating to about $20 million today. Thanks to Katharine's support, in 1960 the birth control pill became available as a very effective contraceptive option.

"Om El-Masriyyin": Mother of the Egyptians

Safiya Zaghloul
(1878-1946)

Safiya Zaghloul was born as Safiya Fahmy in Cairo, Egypt. Her father was the seventh minister of Egypt. When she was eighteen years old, she married Saad Zaghloul, a leader of the Wafd Party, which was an influential political party in the 1919 revolution to free Egypt from British rule. Safiya was with him in all his political activities. When the British banished him from his country and sent him to the European island of Malta, then the African island of Seychelles (both controlled by the British at the time), Safiya bravely continued his revolutionary work. She became a central leader in the Wafd party. After her husband was taken out of the country, there was a big rally at her house, which the people called "Beit Al Umma," or "House of the People." Safiya's secretary read this on her behalf from the terrace of the house: "If the British have arrested Saad and his tongue, then his wife and life partner will make God and the homeland witness that she will replace her great husband, and that she considers herself a mother to all those who came out to protest for the sake of freedom." After the speech, someone shouted, "Om El-Masriyyin!" which translates to "Long live the mother of Egyptians!" From then on, she became forever known as the Mother of the Egyptians. Safiya played a key role in the appointment of a new party leader and led demonstrations of women demanding Egypt's independence from the British. She herself became the leader of the Women's Wafd. Safiya remained a dedicated political activist until she retired. Her home is now a museum in Cairo where visitors can learn more about Safiya's key role in an important era of Egypt's political history.

Courageous Political & Workers' Rights Activist

Winifred Carney
(1887-1943)

Maria Winifred Carney, who also went by Winifred Carney, started her life in Bangor County, Ireland. When she was young, her parents divorced and she moved to Belfast, Ireland, with her mother and siblings. Her mother ran a candy shop to support the children. Winifred's first job was as a teacher. In her early twenties, she decided to go to secretarial school. Winifred became one of the first women in Belfast to be qualified as a secretary and shorthand typist. She got a job at a law firm, but it was not long before Winifred wanted more than secretarial work. At age twenty-four, she became involved in co-founding the women's division of the Irish Textile Workers' Union. There she met James Connolly, a union leader. They worked closely together for rights and better working conditions for female factory workers. James Connolly was also the leader behind a rebellion against the British rule of Ireland at the time. Called Easter Rising, with Winifred as his personal secretary, he led an armed revolt in Dublin, Ireland, by Irish who wanted an independent Irish Republic. Connolly was captured and killed. Winifred was captured and went to prison for eight months for her part in it. She became admired for her courage to stand up for what she believed in, even under dangerous circumstances. A British military general was even reported as saying Winifred and other women involved in the rebellion "were the most dangerous women in Ireland" at the time. After she got out of jail, Winifred returned to her trade union work, which she did for most of the rest of her life. She is remembered as a courageous activist dedicated to the Irish people and their workers' rights in Ireland.

A Fighter for Rights
She Would Not Have

Social Changers

Mabel Ping-Hua Lee
(1896-1966)

Mabel Ping-Hua Lee's life began in the Guangdong province of China. When she was four years old, her father was allowed to move to the United States as a Christian missionary. At that time, only a small number of Chinese people with certain occupations were allowed to enter the country. They could not become citizens. At age nine, a scholarship allowed Mabel to go to school in the United States. She and her family moved to Chinatown in New York. As Chinese immigrants, they were discriminated against. A bright student, at age sixteen Mabel got into all-women's Barnard College. She majored in history and philosophy and published feminist essays in Chinese student publications. While in college, the activist in her came out in full force when she helped lead a big parade in New York in support of women's voting rights. Almost 10,000 people attended. Riding a white horse and wearing a sash saying "Votes for Women," Mabel and other women activists made national headlines. She became well-known as someone who was fighting for women's right to vote yet would not be allowed to vote herself. The Chinese Exclusion Act prevented Chinese immigrants from becoming citizens, which meant she could not vote. Even when the 19th amendment gave women the right to vote when Mabel was twenty-four, Chinese women and many women of color still could not vote. Yet Mabel continued her activist work. She also became the first Chinese woman to get a Ph.D. in economics at Columbia University. In her forties, the Chinese Exclusion Act finally ended. Did Mabel finally become a U.S. citizen and vote? It remains unknown. We do know her activism benefitted many women, and for the rest of her life she remained dedicated to the Chinese community.

Godmother of the
Civil Rights Movement

Dorothy Height
(1912-2010)

After being born in Virginia, United States, at age five Dorothy Height and her family moved to Pennsylvania, United States. Growing up she went to racially integrated schools. Showing leadership skills from a young age, Dorothy became the leader of the Girl Reserve Club, which was a part of the Young Women's Christian Association (YWCA). When she was not allowed to swim in the YWCA pool, she tried to change this rule. She was not successful, but little did she know how she would change the YWCA in the future. A star student, Dorothy got a scholarship to Barnard College, but couldn't go because it did not allow black students. Instead, she went to New York University, got a bachelor's degree in education and a master's degree in psychology. Dorothy then did postgraduate work in social work at Columbia University. Her first job was as a social worker in Harlem, New York. At age twenty-five, Dorothy went to work for the YWCA there and soon became a leader in this organization. Over the next forty years, she did great work to racially integrate the YWCA there and nationwide. Dorothy was also the president of the National Council of Negro Women for forty years. She worked closely with Dr. Martin Luther King Jr. and other civil rights leaders to end segregation. Dorothy received many honors, including the Congressional Gold Medal and an estimated twenty-four honorary degrees. Known for her signature hats, many made by black hatmakers, at age ninety-eight, Dorothy got her wish to be remembered "as someone who used herself and anything she could touch to work for justice and freedom." She has been admired as the "Godmother of the Civil Rights Movement."

Servers of the
Public Good

Opening Doctorate Degree Doors & More

Elena Cornaro Piscopia
(1646-1684)

Unusually smart from a young age, Elena Cornaro Piscopia was born in Venice, Italy, into a wealthy family. Her father encouraged her academic study very early in her life. By the time she was seven years old, she was already skilled in seven languages. In her teens, she studied math, physics, astronomy, linguistics, philosophy, and theology. She even played the harp, harpsichord, and violin. At age twenty-three, when she brilliantly translated a book by a known Catholic monk from Spanish to Italian, word spread, and Elena was invited to be part of scholarly societies of the time. Soon she became known as the most educated woman in Italy. Elena's philosophy instructor inspired her to go further and pursue a doctorate degree in theology. When the local Cardinal of the Catholic Church learned of this, he believed granting her this degree was too close to being ordained as a priest and would not allow it. He did allow Elena to get a doctorate in philosophy instead, which she finished with flying colors. The interest in her thesis defense was so great in the community that it had to be held at a local cathedral to accommodate all the people who wanted to attend! Opening the doors for generations to come, at thirty-two years old Elena became the first recorded female in the world to receive a doctorate degree. She was also very religious and part of the Order of Saint Benedict of the Catholic Church. Before her early death at thirty-eight from tuberculosis, she devoted her final years to serving the needy in society through charity and working with the poor. Her academic achievements and humanitarian contributions remained admired throughout Europe during her day and live on.

Founder of Kindergarten
in the United States

Elizabeth Peabody
(1804-1894)

Elizabeth Peabody's life started in Massachusetts, United States. Her father was a dentist, and her mother was a schoolteacher. At one point when she was a girl her mother also began teaching school in their home to bring in more income. Her mother had a new teaching approach that focused more on drawing students out than just presenting information. Curriculum included subjects like language, literature, theology, philosophy, and history. Her mother's teaching approach would benefit Elizabeth later in the most significant period of her life. As an adult, she first worked as a teacher herself. In her mid-thirties, Elizabeth opened a bookstore and ran it for eleven years before going back to teaching. During this time as a teacher, she also worked to promote public education. In her fifties, Elizabeth learned of a man named Freidrich Fröbel, who had invented kindergarten in Germany. He had developed an educational approach based on organized play, the use of hands and senses, and being involved with nature. It also emphasized that disciplining children should not be based on fear. After trips to Europe to fully learn his approach, Elizabeth decided to devote the rest of her life to writing and lecturing on kindergarten and training kindergarten teachers. At age fifty-five, she opened the United States' first formal kindergarten in Boston, Massachusetts. She passionately sought out people in positions of power around the country and wrote many articles and several books on kindergarten. She became largely responsible for the spread of kindergarten in the United States and its acceptance as an institution in American education. When Elizabeth died, her friends opened the Elizabeth Peabody House to carry on her work. It is still in operation today.

Making History in the Law

Charlotte Ray
(1850-1911)

Charlotte Ray was born in New York, United States, to a reverend father. He was also an important person in the movement to end slavery. He made sure she and her six siblings got a very good education; in the 1860s, the family moved to Washington, D.C., and Charlotte went to the Institution for the Education of Colored Youth, one of the only schools that taught young black women. After graduating, she worked as a teacher at Howard University, which accepted male and female students of all races. There she decided she wanted to practice law and studied it at this university. By age twenty-two, Charlotte became the first black woman to receive a law degree from an American law school. It is not totally clear how she was admitted to the bar of the District of Columbia. Some say she knew that women weren't allowed on the bar of the District of Columbia where she wanted to practice, but applied and took her bar exams anyway as "C.E. Ray" to disguise her gender. Other historians say the bar had already started to allow women. In any case, Charlotte became the first black female lawyer in the United States and the first female to be admitted to the District of Columbia Bar. One of very few women who practiced law then, *Woman's Journal* magazine named her one of the "Women of the Century." Charlotte had her own law practice and became a widely respected corporate law attorney. Despite this, she eventually could not get enough clients who wanted a black woman to represent them and returned to teaching. Charlotte's legal achievements opened the door for women of all races to pursue and practice law.

Founder of the Girl Scouts in the United States

Juliette Gordon Low
(1860-1927)

Juliette Gordon Low, or Daisy as many called her, was born into a wealthy family in Georgia, United States. From an early age, she had an adventurous spirit. In her teens, in school she joined a secret group called Theta Tau that earned badges. Little did she know this would sure relate to her future. Juliette also did things girls weren't supposed to do then, like hiking, playing tennis, and riding horses. Yet in her mid-twenties, she did what was expected of her and married a wealthy man. When she was forty-five, he died, and she lost much of her wealth. Juliette decided to travel and went to France, Italy, Egypt, and India. In her fifties, she was in England and met a British general and war hero, Robert Baden-Powell, who was the founder of the Boy Scouts. She loved the idea of the Boy Scouts, and when he told her about the Girl Guides, which was like the Boy Scouts but for girls, she was inspired to create groups, or patrols as they were called, in Scotland and London. Then she returned to the United States, renamed the Girl Guides the Girl Scouts, and began building this educational and service organization. By age sixty, Juliette was growing the Girl Scouts around the world. In her sixties, she got breast cancer but kept working to support the Girl Scouts until she died. Years later, the Girl Scouts live on, in Juliette's words, "to help girls live a life of courage, confidence, and character." Juliette was inducted into the National Women's Hall of Fame and received the Presidential Medal of Freedom. Her birthplace is a National Historic Landmark, and she is buried in her Girl Scout uniform!

Founder of the Social Work Profession

Jane Addams
(1860-1935)

Tragedy struck early in Jane Addams' life. Born in Illinois, United States, at two years old, her mother died. At four years old, Jane got tuberculosis of the spine, which led to health problems for the rest of her life. Jane found comfort in reading. She became interested in the poor from reading Charles Dickens' stories. She wanted to become a doctor to help the poor. Jane got her bachelor's degree, but her health problems kept her from finishing medical school. At age twenty-seven, Jane found a way to help the poor without becoming a doctor. She learned about places called settlement houses, which provided services to the poor, which were mostly immigrant families then. When she and her friend Ellen Star visited one in London, they became inspired to open one themselves. They founded Hull House, which became one of the most famous settlement houses in America. Different than traditional charities, people from different economic and ethnic backgrounds came there for help, including education, childcare, healthcare, and recreation. Hull House also pioneered sociological research on inequality and the effects of poor working conditions. Jane became known as the founder of social work as a profession through her Hull House and civic work. For years, Jane was also a passionate peace activist. At age fifty-five, the International Congress of Women chose her to head a commission charged with finding an end to World War I. Jane received the first honorary master's degree from Yale University and wrote books on Hull House, social ethics, and peace. At seventy-one, Jane became the first American woman to be awarded the Nobel Peace Prize for her life-long commitment to the poor and social reform.

The Earth's Lawyer

Polly Higgins
(1968-2019)

Polly Higgins was from Glasgow, Scotland. Her parents were both environmentally minded, and there were many discussions in their home about climate issues. After college and graduate work, Polly went to law school in London, at age thirty passed the bar, and began practicing corporate and employment law. At the end of one big case, she found herself thinking about the harm being done to the earth and how there was not enough being done about it. "The earth is in need of a good lawyer," she thought to herself. Polly made a bold move. She gave up her high-paying job and sold her house to focus on creating a global law called "ecocide law." It seeks to protect the earth from harm by making business and government leaders criminally liable for the damage they do to ecosystems. The law also protects people. Ecocide leads to the destruction of resources, which results in war, so can be seen as a crime against peace. Polly founded the Earth Law Alliance, Earth Community Trust, Earth Protectors fundraising group, and co-founded Ecological Defense Integrity. She wrote *Eradicating Ecocide* and *Earth is our Business* and gave many lectures at conferences and universities. There is a documentary about her work called *Advocate for the Earth*. Polly received an honorary doctorate from Business School Lausanne, in Switzerland, and became an honorary professor at Oslo University in Norway. At age forty-two, Polly lobbied at the United Nations Law Commission to recognize ecocide as an international crime. Tragically, at age fifty she died from cancer before ecocide could be formally recognized. Many environmental lawyers, activists, and legal experts remain dedicated to achieving this goal that Polly started on behalf of protecting her client, Mother Earth.

Stars of the
Screen & Stage

First Lady of American Cinema

Lillian Gish
(1893-1993)

Lillian Gish started life in Ohio, United States. Her father was a salesman and her mother an actor. At a young age, her father abandoned the family. She got exposed to acting early when her mother took acting jobs to support Lillian and her younger sister. They moved to Illinois, and she and her sister started acting in school plays. Her mother opened a candy and popcorn shop next to a movie theater, but when it burned down they moved to New York. There she made friends with a child actor who lived next door. Through her, Lillian and her sister met silent film director D.W. Griffith, who helped them get contracts with one of the top motion picture companies at the time. During the next two years, Lillian was in twenty-five short films and feature films. She became a well-known silent film star. Lillian went on to make over seventy-five silent films. Often playing the lovely heroine who suffers yet shows inner strength, she mastered techniques that had great emotional impact. Lillian also did anything to get the right shot. In one film, acting unconscious, she floated on ice toward a waterfall. Because of the many seriously cold takes, she had pain in her right hand for the rest of her life. When the silent film era turned to talking films, Lillian did not slow down. She was in over twenty films and many TV movies and series episodes. Lillian also became an accomplished theater actor and performed in seventeen plays. She did her last film at the age of ninety-four and gave one of the best performances of her career! Lillian received many honors for her acting achievements and remains known as the "First Lady of American Cinema."

Queen of Hollywood Costume Design

Edith Head
(1897-1981)

Edith Head was from California, United States. At age eight her parents divorced, her mother remarried a mining engineer, and they lived in mining camps in the Western United States and Mexico. As a child, she learned how to sew. After high school, Edith got a bachelor's degree in French from UC Berkeley and a master's degree in romance languages from Stanford University. After teaching French and Spanish, she became frustrated about being underpaid. Edith was also interested in design and studied at Chouinard Art Institute in Los Angeles. In her mid-twenties, Edith saw an ad for a costume sketch artist at Paramount Pictures, one of the leading Hollywood studios at the time. She borrowed other students' sketches for the job interview. Paramount hired her not knowing the sketches weren't hers, but it still turned out to be a smart move. Edith started as an assistant designer, and after ten years got promoted to designer. Five years later, she became chief designer and was the first woman in the film industry to ever have this job. During her career, Edith did costumes for more than 1,100 films and became one of Hollywood's leading costume designers. She had a to-the-point personality, and actors loved her because she valued close relationships with them, gave them what they wanted while designing the costumes to fit the film character. Edith's almost sixty-year career brought her thirty-five Academy Award nominations and eight awards for Best Costume Design. At seventy-seven years old, she got a star on the Hollywood Walk of Fame. She wrote two books on her career and 'less is more' design philosophy. Edith remains one of the leading costume designers in film history.

Gifted Method Actor Who Did Hollywood Her Way

Greta Garbo
(1905-1990)

With the given name of Greta Lovisa Gustafsson, she was born into a poor family in Stockholm, Sweden. While shy as a girl, Greta loved making up performances with her friends. At age fourteen her father died, and instead of finishing high school, she had to get a job. She worked in a barber shop, then at a department store. After being in women's clothing commercials for the store, Greta got a scholarship to Stockholm's Royal Dramatic Theater Academy. There she met a leading director of Swedish silent movies. She left the Academy to star in one of his movies, which was a success. Now her mentor, he gave Greta the last name of "Garbo." At age twenty, one of the heads of the famous MGM film company saw Greta on screen and offered her the chance to come to Hollywood. In just two years, Greta became a silent film superstar. Unlike many actors, she successfully transitioned to talking films. The public loved her accent and husky voice. Greta is known for bringing "Method" acting to the screen. She was gifted at deeply becoming her characters and expressing their innermost feelings through subtle movements and her eyes. Greta's magnetic performances made her one of Hollywood's greatest actors. But she refused to act like it in real life. Fiercely private, she rejected Hollywood culture. Avoiding publicity made her mysterious and surprisingly resulted in her becoming one of the most publicized women in the world. Contrary to the myth that Greta was a loner, she had many friends. Greta's performances in twenty-eight films brought her many honors, including an Honorary Academy Award and her home country's Illis quorum, a gold medal for outstanding contributions to Swedish culture, science, or society.

YOUR SHOW OF SHOWS

One of Television's First Comics

Imogene Coca
(1908-2001)

Of Spanish and Irish descent, Imogene Coca was born to a father who was a violinist and band leader in Pennsylvania, United States. Her mother worked as a dancer and magician's assistant. As a child, she spent a lot of time with them in the theaters where they worked. She also started piano, singing, and dance lessons at an early age. In Imogene's teens, she was already performing as a song-and-dance girl. By age seventeen, she had moved to New York and made her debut dancing in a Broadway musical. She performed in musicals and musical-comedy shows into her thirties. But it was in her forties when she put her musical, dance, and comedic skills together that she did the biggest show of her career. Imogene starred in the very popular Saturday night television show, *Your Show of Shows*. It had dancing, singing, and guest star appearances, but it was Imogene and her partner Sid Caesar's genius comic skits that made millions of viewers tune in. Imogene was most famous for her pantomimes and the many hilarious ways she could use her face. From 1950 to 1954, Imogene did 160 live *Your Show of Shows*. She won Emmy and Peabody awards for her talents on this show. After this show ended, she continued to perform into her seventies. When Imogene was sixty-four, she was in a serious car accident and became blind in one eye but did not let it stop her. She did the Broadway musical comedy, *On Twentieth Century*, and ended up being nominated for a Tony award for her role in it. At age eighty, she received the Lifetime Achievement Award at the American Comedy Awards. Imogene made millions laugh and inspired many famous female comedians who came after her.

ACTRESS COMEDI SINGER

A Multi-Talented Performer
We Lost Too Soon

Madeline Kahn
(1942-1999)

After being born Madeline Wolfson in Massachusetts, United States, her parents divorced when she was very young. Madeline moved to New York with her mother who wanted to be an actress. Her mother sent Madeline to a boarding school while she pursued this dream. Her mother remarried a man who adopted Madeline. In high school, she started acting herself and was in school productions. She got into college on a drama scholarship. While in college, she earned money as a singing server at a Bulgarian restaurant, where she got experience singing musical comedy. Although a college teacher thought her natural speaking voice would be a handicap, Madeline would prove her wrong. While she got a degree in speech therapy, in her twenties she decided to pursue acting and singing. She would do both for thirty years. Madeline was in twenty-nine films and over twenty theater roles on Broadway, Off-Broadway, and performance concerts. She also did television, including movies and over eighty episodes on the popular *The Cosby Show* as the oddball neighbor. Madeline became best known for her work with the famous director, Mel Brooks. His movies are known for their satire and humor, and Madeline's acting and singing masterfully delivers. Her performance in Brooks' *Blazing Saddles* was put as #74 out of 100 of the greatest performances of all time by the famous magazine, *Premier*! With Madeline's many award nominations, a Tony Award, and being in the American Theater Hall of Fame, Brooks beautifully sums her up: "She is one of the most talented people that ever lived…either in stand-up comedy, or acting…you can't beat Madeline Kahn." When she died of cancer at only fifty-seven, her many admirers sadly expressed she and her talents left us too soon.

Historic Superheroine in Black Action Film

Tamara Dobson
(1947-2006)

Tamara Dobson's life began in Maryland, United States. Her father worked for the railroad and her mother owned a beauty salon. As a girl, her parents worked hard to be able to give Tamara piano, tap, and ballet lessons and send her to private school. By the time she was sixteen, like her mother, Tamara got her beautician's license. She quickly found it boring. At twenty-one years old, she graduated from art school with a degree in fashion illustration. A department store executive introduced her to a designer in New York, she moved there and began modeling and taking acting classes. In her twenties, Tamara appeared in many top magazines, including *Vogue, Essence*, and *Mademoiselle*. She also did television commercials for Revlon, Fabergé, and Chanel. This all changed when she started auditioning for films. At age twenty-five, she got the lead role of Cleo in the black action films *Cleopatra Jones* and *Cleopatra Jones and the Casino of Gold*. In these films, she made film history as the first black superheroine in a new film genre of the time called "blaxploitation." This genre focused on producing films using black actors and appealing to black audiences in a time when Hollywood did not. Nothing like the stereotypical role of black women in film then, Tamara's role as Cleo is a black female version of James Bond. Cleo is a tough undercover agent who drives a Corvette, is a motorcycle daredevil, an excellent markswoman, and a karate master (she had a black belt in real life) who outsmarts her attackers. Her unusually tall height inspired one of the film's headlines: "6 feet 2 inches of dynamite." Tamara as the strong, empowered Cleo holds an important place in the history of portrayals of black women in action cinema.

Masters of Story

First Woman to Win the Pulitzer Prize for Fiction

Edith Wharton
(1862-1937)

Edith Wharton's life began in New York, United States. Her family became very well-off from shipping, banking, and real estate businesses. Edith was a bright and creative child. Even before she could read, she made up and told stories. She was educated by tutors and taught herself by reading in her father's library and libraries of her father's friends. At age eleven she tried to write her first novel, and in her teens wrote poetry. By the age of fifteen, she had written her first novella (a short novel). In her twenties and thirties, she fulfilled her duties as a social elite but did not like it. It did serve her creatively, though. Edith would use her experience of the New York upper-class world in her novels. At age forty-three, she published the novel, *The House of Mirth*, which tells a tale of a loss from life of privilege and criticized the realities of the upper class. This book sold well and made her known as an author who took readers into the lives of New York elites. In her mid-forties, Edith moved to Paris and loved mingling with artists and writers there. From 1912 to 1920, she wrote more novels, but her book, *The Age of Innocence*, is the one that stands out. Published in 1920, it gives a picture of New York high society in the 1870s. At age fifty-nine, Edith became the first woman to receive the Pulitzer Prize for Fiction for *The Age of Innocence*. It has since been adapted for film, theater, and television. In her life, Edith published more than fifty books and was awarded an honorary degree from Yale University.

Brilliant Children's Story Writer Who Died a Horrific Death

Else Ury
(1877-1943)

From a family of merchants, Else Ury was born in Berlin, Germany. Her mother was educated and encouraged Else and her siblings to learn literature, arts, and music. She went to good schools through the tenth grade and did well. Else was drawn to writing and began working under a fictitious name for a local newspaper. She loved writing children's stories and fairy tales and became known as the "Lady of Fairy Tales" for young people's magazines. In her late twenties, she published her first book, a collection of thirty-eight tales. While the young adult novels of her time told stories of girls growing up and getting married, Else's characters were able to do the same things as their brothers. By her thirties, she had published her most popular series of stories called the *Nesthäkchen*, translated "baby of the family," for readers twelve to sixteen years old. It follows the main girl character from childhood to old age. Else wrote more than thirty books, and readers loved her smart, funny, and compassionate stories. She sold millions of copies between the years 1918 to 1933 and was considered one of the most successful female writers of her time. Else's career ended, though, when World War II started. When Jewish German children packed their bags to flee Germany, their *Nesthäkchen* books had to go with them. When these children became mothers and grandmothers, they passed them on to the next generations. Else was also Jewish, was barred from publishing, and at age sixty-six was sent to the concentration camp, Auschwitz, and killed in the gas chamber. Despite this horrific end of her life, after the war, Else's books that got smuggled out were re-released, helping her great works to live on.

Taking the Short Story Genre into a New Era

Katherine Mansfield Beauchamp
(1888-1923)

Katherine Mansfield Beauchamp was from Wellington, New Zealand, and was born into an extended family of politicians, businessmen, and writers. She showed an interest in writing from an early age. At the age of twelve, Katherine published her first short story, "His Little Friend," in a New Zealand magazine. In high school, a piece by her in the school's magazine had a note from the editor saying she showed "promise of great merit." He would be right. While in college in London she wrote so well for the school newspaper she became its editor. After college, she was determined to become a professional writer. In London, she became friends with other writers, philosophers, and artists. Writing under the name Katherine Mansfield, her writing would take the short story into a new era. Using story plot and narrative in new ways, her writings had a range of relatable themes, including family challenges, sexuality, relationships, critiques of upper classes, and finding meaning in a difficult world. Her brother was killed in World War I, and this loss also inspired stories based on memories of New Zealand. During her lifetime, Katherine published collections of short stories, many poems, and reviews in literary journals. Tragically, at the age of thirty-four, she got tuberculosis and died. Shortly before her death, she wrote some of her best short stories. After she died, several of her unfinished works were published and have been translated into many languages. Schools and parks in New Zealand have been named after Katherine, her birthplace has been preserved as the Katharine Mansfield House and Garden, and there are films and television shows about her. Katherine is regarded as one of the most influential authors of the 19th and early 20th centuries.

Queen of Crime

Queen of the Crime Novel

Elizabeth Mackintosh
(1896-1952)

From Inverness, Scotland, Elizabeth Mackintosh showed an interest in writing as a girl. In high school, she wrote short fiction and poems. She went to a physical training college and became a physical education teacher. Elizabeth taught for eight years in Scotland and England before returning to Inverness to take care of her father after her mother died. This is when she began her career as a writer. By her early twenties, Elizabeth had published short stories and poems in Scottish newspapers and the literary magazine, *The English Review*. At age thirty-three, she published her first mystery novel, *The Man in the Queue*, under the fictitious name, Gordon Daviot. It is not known why she chose Gordon, but Daviot was a place she loved in her youth. Elizabeth went on to write a series of suspenseful crime novels, one under the Daviot name, and the rest under Josephine Tey, her great-great-grandmother's name. With Inspector Alan Grant as the main character in the series, the best known is *The Daughter of Time*. Elizabeth was introverted, and many people felt she was hard to get to know. It's been said that the characters in her novels give us clues about her. Some of those who have studied her work also see Inspector Grant as her alter ego. For example, he is Scottish, a bachelor who, like her, saw marriage as a loss of freedom. Elizabeth also wrote many plays under the Daviot name. One play, *Richard of Bordeaux*, ran for hundreds of performances in London. Since her death, Elizabeth's plays have been featured on radio and television. In 1990, the Crime Writer's Association named her book, *The Daughter of Time*, the best crime novel ever written.

A Driving Force in Mid-20th Century Children's Books

Margaret Wise Brown
(1910-1952)

Margaret Wise Brown started her life in New York, United States. An imaginative and adventurous child, she was educated in private schools in Switzerland and Massachusetts. At twenty-two years old, Margaret received her bachelor's degree in English from Hollins College (now Hollins University) in Virginia. Thinking she might want to become a teacher, she completed a teacher training program on "Here and Now" children's literature. This style espouses that young children don't like fairy tales or fantasy nursery rhymes as much as stories that encourage them to explore their real environments and experiences. At twenty-seven years old Margaret published her first children's book, *When the Wind Blew*. The publisher was so impressed with her "here and now" style that they hired her as a children's book editor. By the time she was thirty-one years old, her own children's books were so successful she quit her job as an editor and focused on writing full-time. Children and those reading to them loved her simple, rhythmic writing that peaked children's senses and told stories of getting lost and found, being alone then once again protected. In addition to publishing books under her own name, Margaret used fictitious names as well, including Timothy Hay, Golden MacDonald, and Juniper Sage. Collaborations with some of the most respected illustrators at the time were also very important to the success of her books. By the time she died suddenly at the age of forty-two, Margaret had written more than one hundred books! Two that remain classics today are *Goodnight Moon* and *The Runaway Bunny*. In 1990, seventy more unpublished manuscripts were found and published. Margaret's books and biographies written about her keep her legacy alive as an evolutionary force in modern children's books.

Gifted Modern Chinese Literature Writer

Eileen Chang
(1920-1995)

Shanghai, Chinese-born Eileen Chang's birth name was Zhang Ying. She started school at age four and was educated bilingually. Before starting an English school at age ten, her mother renamed her Àilíng, translated as Eileen. Also at age ten, her parents divorced, and she lived with her father. While in boarding high school, she loved Chinese literature and showed talent with writings published in the school magazine. When she was eighteen, Eileen got dysentery (illness in the stomach and intestines), which forced her to stay in her bedroom for six months. Eileen went to live with her mother after that. She got a full scholarship to the University of London, but couldn't go, as it was during World War II. Eileen studied English Literature at the University of Hong Kong for two years, but a Japanese attack on the city forced her to go to Shanghai, where she started making a living writing short fiction and essays. At age twenty-three, Eileen became the most popular new writer in Shanghai. Between 1943-1945, some of her most admired works came out, including *The Golden Cangue, Love in a Fallen City, Romances*, and *Written on Water*. With literary maturity beyond her age, Eileen's books portrayed the lives of ordinary men and women in 1940s Hong Kong and Shanghai, a time of social change and war. Her works were banned in mainland China because two of them criticized Communists. Eileen's books were later semi-autobiographical of her early life struggles. Eileen had huge Taiwanese and Chinese followings around the world. By the 1970s, her work was available in mainland China. Several of her books and stories were made into movies, including *Lust, Caution*, directed by Ang Lee. Eileen's body of work remains important to modern Chinese literature.

Blockbuster Gothic Horror Novelist

V.C. Andrews
(1923-1986)

Cleo Virginia Andrews, better known as V.C. Andrews (Virginia C. Andrews), was born in Virginia, United States. In her early teens, she got rheumatoid arthritis, a painful condition, that was not solved with surgeries. She had to use crutches and a wheelchair. V.C. had artistic talent, and after completing a four-year course, she became a successful commercial artist. She became inspired to write later in life. She typed standing up in a body brace at a chest-high desk or in bed. At the age of fifty-six, V.C. published the first in a trilogy of gothic horror novels, *Flowers in the Attic*, which topped the bestseller lists in just two weeks. Each year after that for seven years she published a new novel with bigger advances and growing fans. The second in the trilogy is *Petals on the Wind*, and the third *If There Be Thorns*. *My Sweet Audrina*, *Seeds of Yesterday*, *Heaven*, and *Dark Angel* followed. The seven novels made the bestseller lists and have sold millions of copies. V.C.'s stories are an absorbing mix of Gothic horror and family dramas. Tragically, at the age of sixty-three, V.C. died of breast cancer. By the time of her death, her books had made $24 million in sales, and she had been named the Number One Bestselling Author of popular horror and occult paperbacks by the American Booksellers Association. Her publisher wanted to keep her work alive and found a ghostwriter to write more books under her name. It would be six years before the ghostwriter's identity would be known. The ghostwriter kept her phenomenon going and published over seventy books in V.C. Andrews' style. It has grown into an empire, selling over a hundred million copies all over the world!

Visionary Sci-Fi Writer

Octavia Butler
(1947-2006)

The shy daughter of a housekeeper and shoeshiner, Octavia Butler was born in California, United States. When her father died as a child, she lived with her mother and grandmother. Octavia started writing stories as early as age ten. Loving to use her imagination, she started writing sci-fi in her early teens. Despite being told by her aunt that "Negroes can't be writers," Octavia was passionate about doing so. After getting an associate degree, she supported herself with odd jobs while studying creative writing at California State University Los Angeles, the Screen Writers Guild Open Door Program, and the Clarion Science Fiction Writers' Workshop. In her twenties, Octavia developed her writing skills. After a series of rejections, she published her first novel, *Patternmaster,* when she was twenty-nine. Critics loved it. Octavia went on to write the Patternist, Xenogenesis, and Parable series, two standalone novels, *Kindred* and *Fledgling,* and short stories. All were very successful, but *Kindred* has remained her bestseller. Octavia's stories are known around the world to have an amazing combination of science fiction, fantasy, horror, humanity, political and social commentary, often with female black main characters. She received many awards, including being in the Chicago State University's International Black Writers Hall of Fame and the first sci-fi writer ever to get the esteemed MacArthur Fellowship. Octavia's reputation is still very much alive. Her stories include the future of U.S. politics and climate change, which surprisingly ring true today. *Kindred* has been made into a television series, and she would be thrilled to know there is even an asteroid named after her.

Movement & Melody

Gifted Ballerina Who Died Too Soon

Anna Pavlova
(1881-1931)

Anna Pavlova was born in St. Petersburg, Russia. As a child, although poor, her mother was able to take her to *The Sleeping Beauty* ballet at the famous Mariinsky Theatre. She loved what she saw so much she decided then and there she wanted to become a ballerina. Her mother was very supportive, and the next year, helped Anna be able to audition for the Imperial Ballet School. The school rejected her because of her youth, but the next year accepted her. At age eighteen, Anna graduated from this school as a leading dancer. Quickly seen as a gifted young ballerina, that same year she made her debut in *La Fille Mal Gardée* (The Wayward Daughter) at the Mariinsky Theatre—the very place she had fallen in love with ballet for the first time. Her amazing career lasted over twenty years. Anna's breakthrough performance was in *The Dying Swan* when she was twenty-four years old. She was known to have said that watching swans in a park in Leningrad, Russia, inspired her idea to do a swan dance. Anna so beautifully performed the ballet's theme of the fragility and preciousness of life. It was not long before she was promoted to prima ballerina, and by her early thirties, she started her own ballet company. Anna toured her company all over the world. She also had a big heart; when World War I was over, she started a home for Russian orphans and helped dancers in need. Sadly, her career was cut short. At age fifty-one, she got pneumonia and died. Anna was one of the most admired ballet dancers of her time, and her legacy lives on with the many dancers she continues to inspire.

Out of Emotion, Comes Form

The Mother of Modern Dance

Martha Graham
(1894-1991)

Martha Graham began her life in Pennsylvania, United States. By her teens, she and her family lived in California. Her father was a doctor who specialized in nervous disorders, and how he used physical movement as treatment fascinated her. So did seeing her first dance performance in Los Angeles when she was seventeen. Inspired to study dance, after completing an arts-oriented junior college, she went to the Denishawn School of Dancing and Related Arts. Martha studied and taught there for over eight years. By her late twenties, she started her own dance company, the Martha Graham School for Contemporary Dance. Her dance techniques were very different than classical ballet. It requires the body to move in unusual ways that express inner emotions. As she once said, "Out of emotion, comes form." Her most famous works used body movements she termed "contraction and release." Themes of many of her works have to do with the challenges and successes women face. Martha's techniques were criticized at first as strange and even ugly, but over time, they became seen as a major advancement in modern dance. Today the Graham technique is taught all over the world. Over her 50+ year career, Martha created 180 works, and she danced in most of them. She retired at the age of seventy-five, but she choreographed until she died at the age of ninety-six. Close to her death, she was working on a new piece in honor of the 500th anniversary of the discovery of America. It would have been her 181st work. Martha leaves behind a great legacy for dancers and all artists. Her company performs to this day, and she is remembered as the mother of modern dance.

Premier Country Blues Artist

Lizzie Douglas
(1897-1973)

The oldest of thirteen brothers and sisters, Lizzie Douglas was born in Mississippi, United States. When she was eight years old, her parents gave her a guitar as a Christmas present. By the age of ten, she had also learned to play the banjo. Lizzie started playing at parties and was inspired by experienced blues musicians she saw. Wanting to make a life singing and playing music, at thirteen, she ran away from home to Memphis, Tennessee, to do just that. But life was hard; Lizzie started out homeless and had to grow up fast. She started playing in street bands, cafes, clubs, dances, and house parties, and it wasn't long before she started making a name for herself. For a time, Lizzie also joined the Ringling Brothers circus as a traveling musician and toured the South. In her early thirties, a talent scout for Columbia Records discovered her. This launched her recording career. She would go on to record about two hundred songs and become one of the premier blues guitarists, singers, and songwriters of the 1930s and 1940s. She faced racism and sexism, but Lizzie held her own, on and off the stage. She won guitar picking contests with the best of top bluesmen and had a glamorous yet tough stage presence. She could even whistle with the best of them. Considered to be one of the best female blues singers of all time, Lizzie influenced the development of Chicago blues, rhythm & blues, and rock 'n' roll music to come. After her death, she was inducted into the Blues Foundation's Hall of Fame. Adaptations of her songs have been done by many contemporary artists, which keeps Lizzie's music alive today.

Superb Big Band Singer

Anita O'Day
(1919-2006)

With the given name Anita Colton, her life began in Missouri, United States. She grew up during the Great Depression. When she was a child, her family moved to Chicago. Shortly after, her father left, and she was raised by her mother. In her teens, Anita started dancing in marathon ballroom contests. During this time, she changed her last name to "O'Day," Pig Latin for "dough," or money, which is what she wanted to make. She toured the Midwest doing these marathon contests and was occasionally asked to sing. In one contest Anita spent nine days chained to the same dance partner! At seventeen, she stopped doing the marathon contests to pursue becoming a professional singer. After working as a chorus girl, and singer/waitress at Chicago clubs, she got her first big break. At nineteen, Anita started working at a new popular club called the Off-Beat. Three years later, she joined a big band and recorded one of the first interracial vocal duets. The same year, *DownBeat* magazine voted her one of the top big band jazz singers. During her fifty-year career, Anita was known for her original jazz singing style, being gutsy, and her own person. She ditched the standard gowns women singers wore at the time, wearing a stylish skirt and jacket instead. She earned legendary status in her thirties and forties but had her challenges. By her late forties she kicked a heroin habit she writes about in her memoir, *High Times, Hard Times*. In her early fifties, Anita made a comeback and performed until she was eighty-five. She appeared in movies, and there is a documentary about her. Bringing her superb talents and life lessons helped make Anita one of the best jazz singers in history.

The Queen of Salsa

Celia Cruz
(1925-2003)

From poor beginnings in Havana, Cuba, Celia Cruz was the oldest of fourteen children in her home, three of whom were her siblings and the others extended family. Drawn to singing from an early age, she sang the children to sleep at night, performed in school productions and at community events. In high school, winning a singing contest inspired her to pursue it as a career. Thanks to her aunt and a cousin taking her, so did seeing cabaret shows. After high school, she started at Havana's National Conservatory of Music, but professors there convinced her to start her full-time singing career, which she passionately did. In her twenties, Celia got her big break when she became the lead singer and the first black vocalist for Cuba's most popular orchestra called La Sonora Matancera. With her own style of salsa vocals and showy costumes, she performed in many countries and made salsa a more popular style of music. At age thirty-five, Celia was touring in Mexico and the Cuban Revolution was in full force. She decided not to return to Cuba, and the leader of the country at the time, Fidel Castro, banned her from ever coming back. She became an American citizen and the most well-known salsa performer around the world. In her over fifty-year career, Celia recorded more than eighty albums and songs, had twenty-three gold records, and won five Grammy Awards. She was in Hollywood movies and has a star on the Hollywood Walk of Fame. She received honorary doctorates from Yale University and the University of Miami, was awarded the American National Medal of Arts, and was inducted into the International Latin Music Hall of Fame. This Queen of Salsa brought the magic of Latin music to the world.

One of Opera's Greats

Jessye Norman
(1945-2019)

Jessye Norman was born in Georgia, United States, in a serious time of racial segregation and discrimination. Her mother and grandmother were pianists, and her father sang in a local choir. Jessye's parents said she started singing as early as when she started talking. At age four, she began singing gospel at her family's church. When Jessye was seven, she entered her first vocal competition. As a girl, she heard opera on the radio and fell in love with it. She listened to the Metropolitan Opera every Saturday. In junior high school and high school, she took voice lessons. At sixteen she entered another competition, which she did not win, but it led to getting a full scholarship to study music at the black college, Howard University. After graduating, Jessye started graduate study at the Peabody Conservatory, then finished her master's degree at the University of Michigan. In her twenties and thirties, she established her reputation in Europe and made her debut in the United States at age thirty-eight. With a soprano voice like no other, Jessye performed around the world and at major events including presidential inaugurations and Queen Elizabeth II's 60th birthday celebration. She received thirteen honorary doctorates, and her many awards include the famous Kennedy Center Honor, five Grammys, the Grammy Lifetime Achievement Award, the National Medal of Arts, and France's Legion d'Honneur. Jessye also had a big heart. She was a spokesperson for humanitarian issues and started the Jessye Norman School of the Arts, a tuition-free program for students in her hometown. Her memoir, *Stand Up Straight and Sing!*, tells Jessye's story as one of the most popular soprano singers and one of the few black vocalists to attain major fame in the opera world.

Brainiacs

A Star Scientist of 18th Century China

Wang Zhenyi
(1768-1797)

Wang Zhenyi was a famous astronomer and mathematician during the Chinese Qing dynasty in the 1700s. Born in a time when women had no legal rights, she was lucky to be from a family of academics. She learned basic mathematics, medicine, and geography from her father, astronomy from her grandfather, and poetry from her grandmother. At sixteen years old, she taught herself advanced mathematics and astronomy. She also studied traditional Chinese texts and European classics. Outside of academic studies, she also mastered archery and martial arts. Zhenyi saw the need to make it easier for beginners to understand mathematics and astronomy and developed books to do this, such as *The Simple Principles of Calculation*, which had easier ways to do multiplication and division. And she wrote this book at the age of twenty-four! In her life, she wrote a total of twelve books. Most of them were explanations of mathematical theorems. Zhenyi was such a master that she was allowed to tutor male students, which just was not done at the time. One of Zhenyi's most famous discoveries was understanding what causes the lunar eclipse, and she created an experiment to show how it happens when the Moon passes into Earth's shadow. In addition to books, she published articles on her astronomy research. Beyond her scientific work, Zhenyi was also a poet. She wrote thirteen volumes of poetry on subjects like history, the lives of working people, and the rich and the poor. Zhenyi's work also included being a strong advocate for more women to be able to study the sciences. Her brilliance and accomplishments are celebrated with a crater named after her on the planet Venus.

Gutsy Contributor to Mathematical Physics

Marie-Sophie Germain
(1776-1831)

Marie-Sophie Germain was born in France. Her father was a successful merchant and goldsmith, and her mother was the daughter of a goldsmith and friend of philosophers and political economists of the time. When the French Revolution started, she was thirteen years old. With a revolution going on outside, Marie-Sophie had to stay inside. In her father's library, she read about the great mathematician, Archimedes, and decided she wanted to become a mathematician herself. She became so interested in mathematics that she would often forget to eat or drink. Even though her parents were against her becoming a mathematician because women just did not do this at the time, Marie-Sophie taught herself arithmetic, calculus, and even Latin and Greek. When she was eighteen, the school called the École Polytechnique opened in Paris to train mathematicians and scientists. No women were allowed. That did not stop Marie-Sophie. She started corresponding with the most respected mathematicians of the day under the pen name of a man, "Monsieur LeBlanc," about her mathematical theories and calculations. These mathematicians were impressed with 'him' as a mathematician. They eventually found out he was a woman, and this made them respect her even more. In her thirties, Marie-Sophie's third anonymous entry into a competition by the French Academy of Sciences on the theory of elastic surfaces won the grand prize. She explained how elastic surfaces work through mathematical theory. Marie-Sophie's elastic surfaces work had significant applications in mathematical physics, like helping make the construction of the Eiffel Tower in Paris, France, possible. She is also famous for her work proving the French mathematician, Pierre de Fermat's Last Theorem, which became named after her—called the Germain's Theorem. Marie-Sophie was such a brilliant mind of her time!

Great Fossil Finder

Mary Anning
(1799-1847)

Mary Anning is known for her discoveries in the field of paleontology, which is the study of fossils. She was born into a poor family who lived on the Jurassic coast of southern England. When storms came, it caused sea cliffs to fall, releasing rocks with fossils in them. Mary's first big discovery was with her brother when she was twelve years old. He found the skull of a marine reptile called an ichthyosaur, and she found the rest of the skeleton. She was hooked. Mary taught herself geology, anatomy, and paleontology and became very skilled at classifying fossils. She made many major fossil discoveries in her life, such as other ichthyosaurs, the first documented dinosaur, and a flying reptile called a pterosaur. In her early thirties, Mary made one of her biggest discoveries, a Plesiosaurus macrocephalus, the skull and jawbone of a reptile called a plesiosaur. Her discoveries helped scientists study the history of Earth's geology, and she became well respected by what were only men in the paleontology field at the time. Some scientists believe that Mary's discoveries contributed to Darwin's famous theory of evolution. Like many women of the time, during her life she was often not given the credit she deserved for her discoveries. Now Mary is more recognized. Natural history museums in London and Paris have some of her famous discoveries on display. And in 2010, the Royal Society, a scientific academy in the United Kingdom, named her one of the ten most influential women scientists in British history. The greatest fossil finder of her time, natural history museums in London, England, and Paris, France, showcase Mary's spectacular finds. Like they did in her time, Mary's fossil discoveries fascinate people around the world.

Breakthrough Geneticist

Nettie Stevens
(1861-1912)

Nettie Stevens began her life in Vermont, United States. She was very bright from a young age. After high school, she became a high school teacher of zoology, physiology, mathematics, English, and Latin. In her early thirties, Nettie decided she wanted to become a scientist. She got into Stanford University and received her bachelor's and her master's degrees in biology. At age thirty-nine, Nettie moved to Pennsylvania and went to Bryn Mawr College to work on her doctorate in cytology, the study of cells. She received her Ph.D. at age forty-one and accepted an offer to do postdoctoral work there. Three years later, Nettie published a series of papers with a major scientific breakthrough. It was already well known to cytologists that an offspring inherits equal numbers of chromosomes from each of its parents. It was not known how the sex of an offspring was determined. There were different theories. Most scientists at the time believed sex was decided by external factors, such as temperature and nutrition acting on a fertilized egg. They did not believe that sex was decided by chromosomes at the instant of fertilization. Nettie is the one who found that a particular combination of chromosomes—X and Y, were responsible for the sex of an individual. She ended the longstanding scientific debate. Sadly, at the age of fifty, Nettie died of breast cancer. In 1933, a geneticist named Thomas Hunt Morgan (and head of biology at Bryn Mawr College when Nettie made the discovery) ended up with a Nobel Prize that included her breakthrough work. Fortunately, years later Nettie has been recognized for her discovery. Her research remains widely regarded as significantly expanding the field of embryology and genetics.

A Physicist Who Never Lost Her Humanity

Lise Meitner
(1878-1968)

Lise Meitner was from a Jewish family in Vienna, Austria. From a young age, she showed an aptitude for mathematics. After her schooling, she was not allowed to go to college because she was female, but luckily, she was able to get a private education before starting graduate work. She went to graduate school at the University of Vienna. Lise passed her doctoral oral exam with the highest honor, summa cum laude, and at the age of twenty-seven, got a Ph.D. in physics, which was very rare for women at that time. During her career, Lise became the first female full professor of physics at the University of Berlin but ended up being forced to flee Nazi Germany to Sweden. She became part of a team that discovered nuclear fission, a term which she named. Unfairly, Lise was overlooked and not even mentioned for the Nobel Prize in Chemistry, the award going to Otto Hahn, a man with whom she worked for thirty years. Because nuclear fission is what creates an atomic bomb, she was known however for being the "mother of the atomic bomb," which she hated. Lise was against the military use of nuclear fission. Later in her life, Lise and her colleagues received the Enrico Fermi Award, one of the most significant science and technology honors given by the U.S. government. Today she is regarded as one of the most significant women scientists of the 20th century. Element 109, called meitnerium (Mt), an extremely radioactive synthetic chemical element, was named in her honor. To capture her love of physics and its use for only peaceful purposes, the inscription on her tombstone says, "A physicist who never lost her humanity."

A Special Sisterhood

Inventions Galore!

Beulah Louise Henry
(1887-1973)

Born in the United States in the state of North Carolina, Beulah Louise Henry was a direct descendant of one of America's founding fathers, Patrick Henry. Her grandfather was a governor of North Carolina, United States, W.W. Holden. She was a curious and creative child, and by the age of nine, she was already drawing sketches of new things to create. One of Beulah's first ideas was how to make a man's hat automatically tip when he met someone. She went to Queens College and Elizabeth College, both in North Carolina. At age twenty-five, Beulah got her first patent for an ice cream maker that worked more easily than the ones used at the time. The next year she got patents for a new kind of purse and umbrella, both with the great new snap-on cover feature. Beulah spent much of her adult life in New York City. There she was president of Henry Umbrella and Parasol Company and continued to receive patents on her ideas. They were everything from new kinds of dolls for children to improvements to sewing machines and typewriters. Her developments to sewing machines revolutionized this industry. Later in her career, companies hired Beulah to develop products for them. During her life, she received a total of forty-nine patents and came up with over a hundred inventions. You can see why Beulah was known as Lady Edison, after the famous inventor, Thomas Edison! She was one of very few women of her time that made her living as an inventor. A popular quote by her about why she invents things: "I invent because I cannot help myself." In 2006, she was inducted into the National Inventors Hall of Fame.

Electrical Engineer Extraordinaire

Caroline Haslett
(1895-1957)

Caroline Haslett was born and grew up in Sussex, England. She got interested in tools and machinery early in her life through her father, who was an engineer for the railroads. She watched her mother do cleaning, washing, and cooking with no machines to help. At nineteen years old, Caroline got a job at an engine boiler company. Engine boilers were important during World War I at the time. While in this job she decided to become an electrical engineer. Caroline had many accomplishments during her career. She was the first director of the Electrical Association for Women, which taught women about electricity. When she was just twenty-four years old, Caroline got a high-level position with the Women's Engineering Society, which promoted engineering as a profession for women. She also became the first editor of *The Woman Engineer* magazine. She used the magazine to identify from women readers what appliances would be the most useful for the home. During World War II, Caroline advised the British Ministry of Labor on training and equal hiring of women to work in industry. She also worked for important governmental bodies and received many awards. In her thirties, she received the special award, the Commander of the Order of the British Empire, for her leadership roles. In her fifties, Caroline was named a Dame Commander of the Order of the British Empire for her outstanding public service. She also became the first female member of the British Electricity Authority, which named a ship after her. Caroline was an extraordinary leader in getting more women to become scientists and engineers in England. As an electrical engineer, her dying wish was also special: she was cremated by electricity.

Computer Technology Pioneer

Grace Hopper
(1906-1992)

From New York, United States, Grace Hopper's parents supported her curious mind from the start. She wanted to know how things work and would often take things apart and put them back together again. She was smart; Grace received her bachelor's degree in mathematics and physics, and a master's degree and Ph.D. in mathematics from Yale University. She started teaching at Vassar College in New York, but it was not long before she tried to enlist in the Navy during World War II. She was denied because her teaching job was valuable to the war effort. Grace later got in to serve in the Women's Naval Reserve and would go on to have a long and pioneering career in the Navy in computer technology. Grace achieved many innovations, including making technology more user-friendly. Grace received more than forty honorary degrees and many awards. They included the first Computer Science Man-of-the-Year Award, the Defense Distinguished Service Medal, and the first woman to receive the National Medal of Technology given by President Bush. Grace also had a hand in why the word 'bug' became associated with computer glitches. In 1947, while she was working at Harvard on an early computer, a moth was found stuck in it, and Grace has been credited with popularizing the term "debugging." Grace was also a gifted teacher at universities, workshops, and conferences, and inspired young people to learn programming. She was known to have said that of all her computer programming and software development accomplishments, she was most proud of all the young people she trained. After her death, President Obama honored Grace with the Presidential Medal of Freedom, the highest civilian honor in the United States.

Top-Notch Codebreaker

Joan Clarke
(1917-1996)

Joan Clarke started her life in London, England. An excellent student, after graduating from high school she received a scholarship to Newnham College, part of the University of Cambridge that was only for women. She earned a double degree in mathematics with honors. At the time she was denied the degree because Cambridge only awarded them to men. But Joan's brilliance did not go unnoticed. Her academic advisor was one of the top mathematicians at the time and gave her the opportunity to become the only woman to work for the government organization, the Government Code and Cypher School. It was charged to break German radio codes and messages during World War II. During this war, radio communication was an important part of warfare strategy. Radio was used in aerial, naval, and land combat. The messages had to be disguised so enemies could not read them. Codebreakers of the time figured out how to decode the enemies' messages. Because she was a woman, Joan had to start out doing clerical work, but it was not long before her codebreaking talents became known. At twenty-five years old, she started to work with a team of the best codebreaking minds of the time that broke the code that the Germans thought was unbreakable. By her late twenties, she became the department head, and she and her team continued to break enigma codes until the end of the war. They say it is hard to know all of Joan's accomplishments because of the secrets codebreakers keep. One thing for sure, she played an important role in her home country's achievements during World War II, which shortened the war and saved many lives.

Medical Pioneers

Founder of the American Red Cross

Clara Barton
(1821-1912)

Clara Barton was born and grew up in Massachusetts, United States. When she was a girl, her brother fell off a barn roof and was badly injured. For two years, Clara helped nurse him back to health. Little did she know that this would be the beginning of her humanitarian work later in life. Her first career was teaching, which included opening and running the first free public school in the town of Bordentown, New Jersey. It was so successful the male town leaders decided a man now needed to lead her school. Outraged, and not wanting to work for a new male boss, Clara resigned and took a job in Washington, D.C. at the U.S. Patent Office. When the Civil War started in 1861, Clara felt called to help care for the injured soldiers. With no formal training, she ended up serving in sixteen battles with the Union Army, the side fighting for the abolishment of slavery. Clara helped get supplies, prepared meals, assisted surgeons, tended to the wounded, and corresponded with soldiers' family members. Her effectiveness, bravery, and compassion gained the respect of soldiers and medical workers. After the war, President Abraham Lincoln was so impressed he appointed her to a job to find missing soldiers. On a visit to Geneva, Switzerland, Clara discovered the International Red Cross, an international agreement to help victims of war. Seeing its great value, she passionately worked to create the American Red Cross, which she established at age sixty. She served as president until she was eighty-two years old. Clara's books, including *History of the Red Cross* and *The Red Cross in Peace and War*, tell her amazing stories as a Civil War hero and American Red Cross pioneer.

Heroic Nurse, Educator & Humanitarian

Edith Cavell
(1865-1915)

From Norfolk, England, Edith Cavell's father, a reverend, schooled her until she was sixteen years old. Then she went to high school and boarding schools. She was exceptional in French, which would help her get a job later as a governess for a rich family in Brussels, Belgium. After working as a governess until she was thirty years old, her father became ill, and Edith went home to England to care for him. This experience led her to want to become a nurse. After training to be a nurse, Edith worked in hospitals in London. In her early forties, she was offered a chance to become a head nurse at a new nursing school in Belgium. There was no established nursing profession in Belgium at the time, and Edith became known as a founder of modern nursing education there. Seven years later, World War I began. For two years, Edith treated wounded soldiers no matter what country they came from. She also did something very risky during a time of war—with Belgian and French colleagues, she helped over 200 Allied soldiers escape German-occupied Belgium to the Netherlands. The German military caught and arrested them. She was found guilty and executed by a firing squad in 1915. Even though it was legal under international law at the time, many countries were outraged. There are many memorials around the world that remember Edith's heroic nursing and humanitarian work. Films, television series, and even a successful opera celebrate her. On the night before her execution, Edith said, "Patriotism is not enough. I must have no hatred or bitterness towards anyone." These words are on this brave woman's memorial sculpture at Trafalgar Square in London.

Researcher Behind the "Wills Factor" Discovery

Lucy Wills
(1888-1964)

Starting her life in Birmingham, West Midlands, England, Lucy Wills was close to her father who ran a tool business and had a serious interest in science. Her parents made sure she got an excellent education. Lucy attended a British boarding school called Cheltenham College for Young Ladies, which taught female students science and mathematics. She went to Cambridge University's Newnham College and studied botany and geology. When Lucy finished at age twenty-three, she only received a certificate from the university, as it did not give women degrees at that time (but did beginning in 1948). Four years later, Lucy started study at the London School of Medicine for Women, got bachelor's degrees in medicine and science, and became qualified to practice at age thirty-two. She decided she wanted to do medical research, and this took her to India. She was charged with investigating why many pregnant women were suffering from "pernicious anemia," a condition where red blood cells are larger than normal and can result in birth defects. In Lucy's research with monkeys, she found that the cause was a lack of folate, a B vitamin. Her discovery became known as the "Wills Factor," and led to the creation of a manmade form of this vitamin called folic acid. Because of Lucy, we now know that women taking folic acid before and during pregnancy helps prevent birth defects in the baby's brain and spinal cord. Lucy's work has been long recognized by nutritionists and hematologists (who treat diseases that affect blood, bone marrow, and the lymphatic system). A member of the highly respected Royal College of Physicians, in her retirement Lucy continued her anemia and vitamin deficiency research, dedicated to ensuring the health of pregnant women around the world.

Celebrated Mohegan Indian
Tribal Medicine Woman

Gladys Tantaquidgeon
(1899-2005)

Descended from a 17th century Mohegan (also known as "Mohican") tribe leader, Gladys Tantaquidgeon was born in Connecticut, United States. By the young age of five, tribal elders chose her to be schooled in the traditions of Mohegan culture. Gladys was educated in Mohegan tribal spirituality and herbal medicine by tribal grandmothers. She also went to non-Indian schools as a girl but did not graduate from high school. Despite this, at twenty years old, she got into the University of Pennsylvania and studied anthropology. Gladys also deepened her Mohegan medicine training by researching herbal medicine related to East Coast tribes. In her thirties, she worked for the Commissioner of Indian Affairs, where part of her job was to encourage the restoration of ancient tribal practices. Gladys published several books about traditional herbal medicine and healing with plants, including *A Study of Delaware Indian Medicine Practices and Folk Beliefs*, reprinted later as *Folk Medicine of the Delaware and Related Algonkian Indians*. Of her many accomplishments for her people, Gladys educated them on Mohegan ways, their tribal language, its spirituality, herbal remedies, healing, and ceremony. With her father and brother, in 1931 she helped found the Tantaquidgeon Indian Museum, which now is the oldest Indian-run and owned museum in the United States. Gladys received honorary doctorates from the University of Connecticut and Yale University. She played an important role in the Mohegan tribe receiving Federal Recognition in 1994. At age ninety-three, Gladys was elected as the Tribal Medicine Woman of the Mohegan. Her life is featured in a book by her great-niece, *Medicine Trail: The Life and Lessons of Gladys Tantaquidgeon*. Gladys is celebrated as a most special Mohegan Indian tribal Medicine Woman, elder, and as its oldest member—she lived to be 106!

Leaving Her Mark on Neurobiology

Rita Levi-Montalcini
(1909-2012)

Born in Turin, Italy, as a young woman Rita Levi-Montalcini knew she had no desire to become a wife and mother like other women of the day. She wanted to go to college and become a doctor and had to persuade her father to let her do this. And she did. At twenty-seven years old, Rita graduated from medical school and started a specialization in neurology and psychiatry. World War II got in the way, however, and she had to stop her studies. Rita kept studying herself though; she built a laboratory in her bedroom and studied the growth of nerve fibers in chicken embryos. Little did Rita know this would lay the groundwork for important research she would do later in her life. Shortly after the war ended, she got a one-semester research fellowship at Washington University in the United States. It turned into an amazing thirty-year career. She continued chicken embryo research and other studies that led to discoveries about the human nervous system and how to recover damaged neurons. Rita's recognitions for her contributions to science include receiving the National Medal of Science, the highest American scientific honor, and being appointed a Senator for life by the Italian Prime Minister. At age seventy-seven, Rita won the Nobel Prize in Physiology or Medicine along with fellow researcher Stanley Cohen. She was the third woman to be awarded this Nobel prize. At ninety-three years old, and still going strong, she founded the European Brain Research Institute and served as its president until her death ten years later, at the age of 103!

Child Healthcare Revolutionary

Fe Del Mundo
(1911-2011)

Fe Del Mundo was from Manila, Philippines. She had eight brothers and sisters, four of whom either died in infancy or as children. These losses inspired Fe to want to grow up and become a doctor. And did she ever. After getting an associate degree in art at age seventeen, Fe went on to medical school. She graduated with valedictorian honors from the UP College of Medicine at the University of the Philippines. She passed the medical board exam the same year. After she graduated from medical school in her early twenties, Fe got an amazing opportunity. The president of the Philippines offered to pay for her to go to any school in the United States to further her medical education. She chose Harvard University. She also attended Boston University School of Medicine. When World War II broke out, Fe cared for children in camps and makeshift hospitals in her country. After working for twenty years as the head of the Department of Pediatrics at a hospital and medical school, she sold her home to finance the first children's hospital in the Philippines, now known as the Fe Del Mundo Medical Center. Fe ran this hospital until she died. During her career, she made many breakthroughs in children's medicine. She also published the *Textbook of Pediatrics* used in Philippine medical schools. A book about Fe's life was published just before her 99th birthday, called *Dr. Fe Del Mundo: A Beautiful Life*. Fe received so many awards during her career, it takes eight pages to list them! They include the Ramon Magsaysay Award, which is Asia's version of the Nobel Prize. Fe is internationally remembered as a major force in shaping modern child healthcare in the Philippines.

Sky & Star Lovers

Ahead of Her Time Astronomer

Hypatia
(circa 350-415 AD)

With her name meaning "supreme," it is estimated that Hypatia was born in 350 AD. She was the daughter of Theon, one of the most educated men in Alexandria, Egypt. He was a well-known mathematician, astronomer, and keeper of the library of Egypt. She and her father were very close. Hypatia was very bright, and he taught her literature, the arts, science, philosophy, religion, and even public speaking. He also taught her to swim, row, and horseback ride. Unlike most girls of the time, Hypatia did not stay home with the women and girls. She went to listen to her father discuss ideas with other scholars. She followed in her father's footsteps and grew up to be a scholar. Hypatia taught astronomy, geometry, mathematics, and philosophy. As a brilliant astronomer, one of her famous teachings involved the "astrolabe," a device that helps astronomers estimate the distance between the horizon and planets and stars. She also worked on advancing mathematical equations and science. Unlike women then, Hypatia wore the kind of robes that scholars and teachers did. She even drove her own chariot! Unheard of then, she never married and chose to remain a virgin. Hypatia was a follower of a mystical philosophy called Neoplatonism, which was considered pagan during a time of religious conflict between Christians, Jews, and pagans. Her life ended too soon. Hypatia was brutally killed for her beliefs, and some say also because she was not married and held such a high intellectual place in society as a woman. Ahead of her time as a woman scholar, Hypatia's spirit lives in space, on a lunar crater on the Moon named in her memory.

Achiever of Firsts in the Field of Astronomy

Caroline Herschel
(1750-1848)

Starting her life in Hanover, Germany, at the very early age of ten Caroline Herschel got an infectious disease called typhus. The disease caused vision loss in her left eye and stunted her growth to just four feet three inches tall. Her mother raised her to believe the best thing she could grow up to be was a maid. But Caroline would prove her wrong. Her family was musical, and when she was twenty-two, her brother William took her to England, where he pursued a career as a conductor and she a singer. He also got very into astronomy. William taught Caroline how to study and record observations of astronomical objects, and she helped him do this. She fell in love with astronomy herself and became a significant astronomer in her own right. At age thirty-six, she was the first woman to discover a comet, and by forty-seven she had identified seven others. Caroline became the first woman to get a salary for astronomical work, the first woman awarded the gold medal by the Royal Astronomical Society, and the first woman to publish findings in the Royal Society's scientific journal. In her eighties, she became an Honorary Member of the Royal Astronomical Society and the Royal Irish Academy. At the age of ninety-six, she received the Gold Medal for Science from the King of Prussia. After spending her last years writing her memoirs, Caroline died at the age of ninety-seven, which was highly unusual at that time! Remembered as a pioneer of her time in astronomy, several of the comets she discovered have her name, and her tombstone reads, "The eyes of her who is glorified here below turned to the starry heavens."

Daring & Barrier-Breaking Aviatrix

Bessie Coleman
(1892-1926)

Of black and Cherokee descent, Bessie Coleman was born into a family of sharecroppers in Texas, United States. She worked in the cotton fields from a young age. Bessie was an outstanding math student, and at age twelve, got a scholarship to a Baptist church school. She went to college until her savings ran out, then moved to Chicago, Illinois. While working in a barber shop as a manicurist she heard stories from pilots who were in World War I. Bessie got so inspired she decided to learn how to become a pilot herself. Flight schools in the United States did not allow blacks or women then. Luckily, a black newspaper publisher she met encouraged her to go to flight school in France, and he helped her find a local banker who helped pay her way. At age twenty-eight, Bessie went to France to go to the Fédération Aéronautique Internationale. The next year, Bessie became the first black person and first Native American to get an international aviation license from this school and became the first black woman and first Native American to earn an aviation pilot's license. After doing advanced training and learning exhibition flying, Bessie quickly became famous for her amazing stunt flying performances. By age thirty, people called her the world's greatest woman flier! Also committed to fighting racism, Bessie refused to do shows that did not allow blacks or separated them in the audience. Tragically, at age thirty-four she died in a plane crash due to jammed controls. Bessie inspired so many aviators and received many honors, including being in the National Women's Hall of Fame and the National Aviation Hall of Fame. Each year, black pilots fly over her grave and drop flowers to honor this daring and barrier-breaking woman.

A Global Flying Legend

Amy Johnson
(1903-1941)

Amy Johnson was from the Yorkshire region of England. She was a tomboy who liked competing with the boys at school. After getting a bachelor's degree in economics, she worked as a secretary at a law firm in London. Amy found the job boring and wanted more excitement. Flying as a sport was in the news then, and one Sunday afternoon, she went to an airfield to watch planes take off and land. Fascinated, she started taking flying lessons, and by age twenty-six, Amy was the first British woman with a ground engineer's license and had her pilot's license. She was determined to make flying her career. In those days, it was hard for women to become professional flyers, so she knew she had to do something big to earn her stripes. Her father helped her buy a plane she named Jason, and she set out to fly solo from England to Australia. Until then, she had only flown in England, so this was a huge goal! She did it and became the first woman to do so. The public went wild, and called her "Queen of the Air." Amy went on to make record-breaking global long-distance flights. At age thirty-six, during World War II, she was called to help get planes from factories to air bases. Piloting a flight, Amy went off course in bad weather conditions. Her body was never recovered. To this day what happened remains unsolved. One thing is for sure, Amy's adventurous spirit and determination became a legend. Buildings, aircraft, and roads are named after her. There are films, television shows, radio shows, and books about her (and she wrote several herself). Jason is displayed at the Science Museum in London in honor of her, Britain's most famous aviator.

First American Woman
to Fly in Space

Sally Ride
(1951-2012)

In the first eight years of Sally Ride's life she lived in California, United States. As a girl, for a year she and her family lived in Europe. In Spain she played tennis for the first time and was a natural at it. By age twelve, she was ranked 20th in Southern California for girls aged twelve and under. In high school, she was an excellent student. After taking a human physiology class, Sally decided she wanted to be an astrophysicist. But Sally also had ambitions to become a professional tennis player. While she won big tournaments, majoring in physics won out. She graduated from Stanford University with a bachelor's degree in physics *and* a bachelor's degree in English literature. By age twenty-seven, she had her master's degree and Ph.D. in physics. When the National Aeronautics and Space Administration (NASA) was looking for women to apply to become astronauts, Sally applied. Her career in space lifted off when she was one of six women picked. At the age of thirty-two, she went on her first space flight, the Space Shuttle Challenger, and became the first American woman to fly in space! Sally's second space flight was also on board Challenger. Before leaving NASA at age thirty-six, she had spent over 343 hours in space. After NASA, Sally taught at the University of California and California Space Institute in San Diego. She founded Sally Ride Science, an organization that helps girls and women study science and math. She also wrote children's books about exploring space. Sally received many honors, including the National Women's Hall of Fame and Astronaut Hall of Fame. A year after her death, this trailblazing astronaut, talented physicist, and committed educator received the Presidential Medal of Freedom.

First Indian Woman Astronaut

Kalpana Chawla
(1962-2003)

It was not long after Kalpana Chawla was born in the state of Haryana, India, that her family knew she loved the sky and stars. Bright and curious as a child, she watched twinkling stars for hours. When planes flew over her home, Kalpana ran to the roof to check them out. Her father took her to flying clubs so she could watch planes take off and land. In school, she loved science class, doing pictures of colorful planes in drawing class, and making aircraft models in craft class. Her nickname was 'Monto' but in high school she changed it to 'Kalpana' because it meant 'imagination.' After watching the Viking I spacecraft launch to explore Mars at age thirteen, Kalpana set her sights on studying space. After getting a bachelor's degree in aeronautical engineering, she went on to get her master's degree, and at age twenty-six, she received a Ph.D. in aerospace engineering. Kalpana did research for the United States' National Aeronautics and Space Administration (NASA) before applying for the NASA Astronaut Corps to train as an astronaut. She was accepted at age thirty-three. In 1997, Kalpana went on her first space mission, becoming the first woman of Indian origin to go into space. In 2003, she went on her second mission. She and the crew did many experiments in space, but when the spacecraft re-entered Earth's atmosphere on their return, it exploded. Such a brilliant astronaut's life ended way too soon. After her death, Kalpana received many honors, including the Congressional Space Medal of Honor, the NASA Space Flight Medal, and the NASA Distinguished Service Medal. In honor of this shining star, an asteroid and crater are named after Kalpana, as are scholarship funds to promote and support women in space.

Gratitude

My deep gratitude goes to the following people
who were of great help to me in the development of
A Special Sisterhood!

Brit McGinnis and Nandita Bajaj for their research assistance
Julia Holladay for her creative input and support
Nataliia Tonyeva for her fantastic illustrations
Michelle Datin for her editorial service
Kekoa Vierra, Shivani Mohan,
and the cadre of twentysomethings
for their feedback on illustrations and cover drafts
Lisa DeSpain, as always, for her excellent book
formatting and cover design
Many thanks to all!

About Laura Carroll

Since the year 2000, Laura has studied women without children. As an expert on the childfree choice, her books include *Families of Two: Interviews With Happily Married Couples Without Children by Choice* and *25 Over 10: A Childfree Longitudinal Study.* She is also the author of *The Baby Matrix: Why Freeing Our Minds From Outmoded Thinking About Parenthood & Reproduction Will Create a Better World.* Laura has contributed to textbooks on childfree and childless topics and has been featured on network television, radio, and in many print and digital media publications, including *Fortune, The Guardian*, and *New York Magazine.*

https://lauracarroll.com
Instagram: https://www.instagram.com/lauralcarroll88/
Twitter: @LauraCarroll88
Facebook:
https://www.facebook.com/ChildfreeandBeyond/
https://www.facebook.com/TheBabyMatrix/

About Nataliia Tonyeva

Nataliia Tonyeva is a digital illustrator who lives in California and is originally from Ukraine. She began her creative path in graphic design, and over time realized her heart belongs to illustration. Not limited to a single style, she uses techniques to craft illustrations that are best suited to tell the particular story. Her love of storytelling is inspired by many designers, illustrators, movies, and animations.

https://byakina.com/

Instagram: https://www.instagram.com/asya_byakina_illustration/